GOD'S CALL TO WOMEN

by

Suzanne Nti

Published by

IMPART BOOKS

Copyright © 1996 Suzanne Nti, Love Alight Ministries,
10 Talman Grove, Stanmore, Middx HA7 4UQ

Published 1996 by IMPART BOOKS,
Gwelfryn, Llanidloes Road, NEWTOWN, Powys SY16 4HX

ISBN   1 874155 26 7

To the glory of our Lord and Saviour, Jesus Christ, whom I serve. I
pray that everything written in this book will be in accordance with the
Word of God and the leading of the Holy Spirit.

Printed by BPC WHEATONS LTD, EXETER EX2 8RP

This book examines the place of women in the Body of Christ, the Church. A controversial subject, some may say. Wait till you have read it, for it is an unusual book of real interest.

We live in a male dominated world, the traits of which unfortunately have found their way into the Church. The Bible clearly states that the Church is the 'light and salt' of this earth, but for many years has not been able to define and accept where God has placed women. This has come about, I believe, by interpreting the women's role through various cultures and traditions. Please do not get me wrong. There is nothing wrong with a particular culture or tradition if it is based on the Word of God. Jesus made it clear by saying that 'the traditions of men make the word of God of none effect'.

A lack of biblical knowledge and a misunderstanding of certain scriptures has led a lot of women to settle for the status quo. The void that has been created, due to the lack of women taking their rightful position in the Body of Christ, cannot be filled by men. God had and has a definite purpose for creating women.

The current position of women in the Body of Christ, I believe, is illustrated in Luke 13:10-17. The woman had been twisted and bent over for eighteen years and could not straighten up. Religious tradition, expectations of society and traditions of men have bent women over for years, hindering them from reaching their God-given potential in the Church.

It has been a blessing and a privilege to have witnessed Suzanne's growth in the things of God since her re-dedication in 1986. Suzanne and her husband, Daniel, relocated to the Netherlands where they set up their own business and remained very much on the cutting edge of ministry. On their return to England, they joined Praise Chapel. They have been an asset to me personally and are active involved in the activities of the local body.

In this book, Suzanne is sounding a clarion call to all women and the body of Christ. She is saying as Jesus said **"Should not this woman, a daughter of Abraham, whom Satan has kept bound for eighteen long years be set free ..... from what bound her ?"** (Luke 13:16)

Rev. Kofi Banful
Pastor, Praise Chapel, London

4

Contents

Page   **Chapter**

3   Foreword

5   Contents

6   Preface

8   1   Reaching for the prize.

14   2   Defining the role of women.

23   3   The so-called Scriptural Controversy.

33   4   Old Testament Women of God.

44   5   Jesus Christ broke with tradition.

53   6   Women in the New Testament.

58   7   Who You Are.

64   8   Single Woman, Wife or Mother.

76   9   Women In Ministry and the Church.

85   10   Tension in the Body of Christ.

93   11   Pressing on towards the goal.

105   Notes.
106   Bibliography.
107   Acknowledgement of Sincere Gratitude.
108   Other books published by IMPART BOOKS.
111   Comments on the book.

Preface

There are many questions regarding the role to which God has called Women to play, within the body of Christ and in His kingdom. Many different teachings and arguments are put forward, some out of ignorance, some from a narrow perspective, usually based on tradition, and some with little revelation.

Some of these teachings and arguments have been deliberate, in order to control, intimidate, limit and hold back women from fulfilling the purpose, ideas, dreams and visions that God has for their lives. The reason for this is the lack of understanding about women, the non-recognition of their gifts and talents, and ignorance of what is expected of them in the body of Christ and in His kingdom.

No one respects God's greatest creations, man and woman, more than God Himself. God had a purpose in mind when He created each and every one of us. Rev. Myles Monroe states "Where the purpose of a thing, object or person is not known, abuse is inevitable." (Note 1) 'Abuse' simply means abnormal use.

To find out the actual purpose of a thing, you do not ask the thing itself. The real purpose of a thing is only found in the mind of its creator. Our creator is God and in Him alone is our purpose found.

This book takes a look at what the Word of God says about women and their role in His kingdom. We look at God's unique women in Old and New Testament times and the extraordinary roles they played. We define the role of women in the light of God's word, not according to tradition. We look at women through the eyes of God.

We look at the scriptures relating to individuals as well as to those who are married, husbands and wives. You need to know who you are in Christ Jesus. Do not just accept someone else's opinion. Find out for yourself the role that God has for you to play in the Body of Christ. **"The fear of the Lord is the beginning of wisdom, and knowledge of the Holy one is understanding."** (Proverbs 9:10). Only godly wisdom can help you move in the direction and purpose that God has planned for you.

Once you know His will for you, being courageous comes next. Champions are simply those willing to make very difficult changes in order to taste the ultimate rewards they are capable of pursuing and reaching. Being courageous means that you see the importance of something and nothing stops you from reaching out for it, not even fear. **"For God did not give us a spirit of timidity, but a spirit of power, of love and of self discipline."** (2 Timothy 1:7)

We look at the false doctrines, arguments and scriptures that are taken out of context and used against women. How do we deal with the heavy duty requirements that are imposed on women and which often keep them from fulfilling God's plan and purpose within the Body of Christ ? For what should we look out and how do we avoid getting into difficult situations ? How do we deal with these situations, if we do happen to find ourselves in the middle of one ?

1 Reaching for the prize

As any Christian woman, and in my hunger and thirst for righteousness, there is a desire in my heart to be and do all that I know the Lord has called me to be and do : to study and show myself approved unto God. Some may call it determination, commitment and dedication to the Word of God by a woman. Others choose to call it the spirit of feminism or women's liberalism. The latter description is not what Jesus told Martha, when Mary chose to sit at His feet. Jesus's words **"but only one thing is needed. Mary has chosen what is better, and it will not be taken away from her."** (Luke 10:42)

All I ask is to be what I was meant to be in Christ Jesus. I am not ashamed to say that I want to be a woman of God. More than to please man, I want to please God. As Jesus said **"for they loved praise from men more than praise from God."** (John 12:43) I am out to achieve all that God has for me here on earth. God did not tell me that I could not have it all.

Some may find such behaviour from a woman objectionable, but God does not. As one writer put it, "When it comes to Christianity, identification is the basic issue. Who you are in Christ Jesus. Knowledge of whom you are in Christ is edifying. There is nothing more thrilling than to stand in the righteousness of God and declare your identity with Christ." (Note 2)

Our Lord Jesus told his disciples **"And these signs will accompany those who believe: In my name they will drive out demons; they will speak in new tongues; they will pick up snakes with their hands; and when they drink deadly poison, it will not hurt them at all; they will place their hands on sick people, and they will get well."** (Mark 16:17-18) This promise was made to "them that believe", any man, woman, boy or girl who believes. I quote the phrase that "Christianity is not built on suppression or repression, but on confession". (Note 3)

Why write a book on a controversial topic, many would ask ? Obviously, not to win a popularity contest. This is the vehicle that the Lord has given to me, to reach His body and the world with His message to liberate women for active service.

In 1 Corinthians 12:22-26, the Bible says **"those parts of the body that seem to be weaker are indispensable, and the parts that we think are less honourable we treat with special honour. And the parts that are unpresentable are treated with special modesty, while our presentable parts need no special treatment. But God has combined the members of the body and has given greater honour to the parts that lacked it, so that there should be no division in the body, but that its parts should have equal concern for each other. If one part suffers, every part suffers with it; if one part is honoured, every part rejoices with it."**

No part of the body of Christ should be hurting if we are walking the way that we are supposed to walk.

This book is to bring out the Truth about what the Word of God says about women generally, wives and mothers. To bring light into the dark and grey areas relating to the position and function of women in God's House. It is the Truth that you know that will set you free. Knowledge of the Word of God brings freedom, understanding and deliverance.

"My people are destroyed from lack of knowledge." (Hosea 4:6) Do not allow yourself to fall into the category of those who are being destroyed just for being ignorant. Jesus said **"Then you will know the truth, and the truth will set you free."** (John 8:32)

Each one of us needs to know for ourselves what the Word of God says. In the days of the Old Testament, when they did not have the Bible as we have it today, you see that when the kings, prophets or people did not know what to do or what was required of them by God, they inquired of the Lord. Whenever they did this and followed the instruction of the Lord, they were successful in their endeavours. Do not accept the Word of God second-hand.

Follow the example of the Berean Christians who were commended for their diligence. Acts 17:11 reads **"for they received the message with great eagerness and examined the Scriptures every day to see if what Paul said was true."**

Check out God's Word for yourself. I want everything that God has for me for eternity, starting here on earth. How about you ?

Before I re-committed my life to the Lord Jesus in 1986, my academic achievements were a Bachelors and a Masters degree in Law. I was qualified to be a lawyer. Since then, a lot has happened in my life.

I recall vividly a job interview which I had, while seeking a job as a trainee solicitor. A senior partner of a law firm in London told me bluntly that I had two handicaps. I was surprised by his comment and asked him to explain what the two handicaps were. He said "Well, first of all, you are a woman and, secondly, you are black."

Having grown up in Ghana, with a black father and a white mother, I had never been told that it was a handicap or a hindrance to be black. On the contrary, I was proud to be light chocolate coloured. The whole of Europe spends hours on the beaches just to have such a skin colour. I had never been confronted with colour or sexual prejudice so directly. I felt sorry for the senior partner, but, at the same time, I knew that his attitude would not give me the job.

I thank God for parents who had made me proud of who I was and the colour of my skin. When I came to Jesus, He accepted me in the beloved. He did not make me feel a particular colour, a particular sex or inferior in any way. His love for me was no less than for a male or for a white or black person.

I am a co-heir with Christ.(Romans 8:17). I am a son of God as I am led by the Spirit of God.(Romans 8:14). Strongholds of racism, sexism or any other "ism" must not be tolerated, condoned or allowed into the House of the Lord. They must be prayed out of existence.

There are millions of sisters out there, all over the world, who feel the burning desire and passion to be and do all that the Lord Jesus has called them to do, especially those who are supposed to be in the ministry. The prophet Jeremiah said **"But if I say "I will not mention him or speak any more in his name", his word is in my heart like a fire, a fire shut up in my bones. I am weary of holding it in; indeed, I cannot."** (Jeremiah 20:9)

No matter how hard Jeremiah tried, he was unable to suppress the divine message within him. The prophet felt such a oneness with God and his cause that he had to proclaim God's word, although it brought him excruciating pain and suffering.

Many pray for the fire of the Holy Spirit to come down. They see a manifestation of the power of God. But do they really want to see the fire come down in its fullness ? They want to see it come down but they limit the movement of the Holy Spirit to their rules and boundaries. They do not allow the Holy Spirit to be Lord in the situation. Yes, the Holy Spirit is there, but is He really allowed to be Lord ?

"Where the Spirit of the Lord is, there is freedom" (2 Corinthians 3:17) Christian liberation frees believers for service in the special place that God has purposed for them in the Body of Christ. When people stop limiting the movement of the Holy Spirit, stop discriminating as to the choice of earthen vessel made by the Holy Spirit, and stop using their minds in delegating duties in the local churches, they will see a more powerful, fuller, easier and greater movement of the Spirit of God.

In London, I had the privilege to sit under some wonderful and anointed men and women of God. I praise and thank God for strong godly pastors, who encourage and train both men and women to fulfil their highest calling in Christ Jesus. They are neither threatened nor intimidated by their female counterparts and dare to **"regard no-one from a worldly point of view"**. (2 Corinthians 5:16)

I thank God that I had the privilege of serving on the mission field in the Netherlands. My heartfelt prayer for all saints is that they are not complacent or discouraged by winds of adversity, but that they fan the flame and stir up the gifts, as Apostle Paul told Brother Timothy.

We must put past failures and disappointments behind us and press on for the prize of the high calling that God has for each one of us. Let your gifts work where God wants you to be. Pray for open doors to minister in whatever position you find yourself. If you are a wife and mother and you are wondering what is happening to your ministry, ask God to show you how you can best serve Him in your particular situation and circumstances.

Make use of all the opportunities given to you, wherever you are, to serve the Lord, whether it be singing, encouraging, serving, teaching, writing, cleaning (yes, cleaning) or preaching. Never say "No" to an open door from the Lord. A lot of the time, we find security in the things with which we are familiar: we resist change and new opportunities as they present themselves.

Sometimes God decides to lead us through an open door, to walk in realms that we have never known before. Beyond the open door is a new and fresh anointing. We must walk on through the open door because the Lord will go before us into greater power than we have ever known before. I pray that saints will seek God's wisdom in choosing a local church where they can submit, grow and develop to fulfil God's vision for their life.

Whether God's plan for you is in a secular job, to be a wife and mother, a full-time or part-time preacher, teacher, administrator, musician or serving in any special place within the Body of Christ, you must find this purpose and direction and fulfil it. We must all deal with the giants, strongholds, adversities and obstacles that we have to face in taking the promised land, knowing that **"in all these things we are more than conquerors through him who loved us."** (Romans 8:37)

12

Do not let the devil cheat you into settling for a life of compromise and unfulfillment. We must do all that God has planned for us to do before we meet Him face to face. Jesus gave us **"authority to trample on snakes and scorpions and to overcome all the power of the enemy"**. (Luke 10:19)

Evil influences are at work in our current world system and even in some of our local churches. We need to use the weapons of our warfare to advance the kingdom of God. We need to know what the Word of God says about us. We must not accept half truths, arguments or scriptures taken out of context and made into a false doctrine geared and designed solely to limit, control, or oppress people.

Jesus advised his disciples to be **"as shrewd as snakes and as innocent as doves"** in dealing with religious people. (Matthew 10:16) The same advice applies today to all children of God, especially to women, wives and mothers. You need to know what the Truth is, because it is the truth that will set you free to be who you are supposed to be. What joy, what overwhelming joy, when the King of Kings and the Lord of Lords says the words **"Well done, good and faithful servant !"** (Matthew 25:21)

I thank God for the examples that have gone before me, recorded in the Old and New Testaments. I thank God for all the godly women of our times, too many to mention, whom I respect, admire and for whom I pray. The women who have dared to rise against the odds, to inquire of the Lord, to stand and obey the Word of God and the voice of the Spirit of God. To be and do what God has asked them to be and do for the kingdom.

If you are searching for His Truth and Will concerning yourself, may our God speak to you. May the eyes of your understanding be opened to the truth in His word. I bind that spirit of fear in the name above all names, Jesus Christ. His Word is Truth. I pray that God will give you the wisdom, understanding, revelation, courage, boldness, patience and all that you need to fulfil His plans and purposes for your life.

What place has God got for women in His plan ? What is your role in His kingdom and in the Body of Christ ? You need to find out by reading God's word, the Bible. If you want to find out what inheritance has been left to you by a deceased relative, you have to read his or her Will.

When you become a Christian, you inherit all that God has for you. **"Praise be to the God and Father of our Lord Jesus Christ, who has blessed us in the heavenly realms with every spiritual blessing in Christ."** (Ephesians 1:3) You need to read the Word of God to find out what God has provided for you and promised you in His Word. His Word is His Will.

"My people are destroyed from lack of knowledge" (Hosea 4:6) is a very relevant scripture to God's children in the age in which we live. It is important to know what applies to us. Apostle Paul told Timothy to **"Do your best to present yourself to God as one approved, a workman who does not need to be ashamed and who correctly handles the word of truth."** (2 Timothy 2:15)

The consequence of the ignorance, from which many Christians suffer, is clearly illustrated by a classic story. A man saved up his money and bought a ticket for an expensive three-week boat cruise. During the once-in-a-lifetime cruise, he had a wonderful time during daytime. He strolled on the deck, took in the sun, swam, and involved himself in all the other activities that were available on deck.

However, his evenings were rather lonely. Each night, as he walked to his cabin, he beheld a beautiful sight. He passed by a magnificent banqueting hall, filled with nicely dressed people, all having a wonderful time. They were helping themselves to the sumptuously laid out dishes on the banqueting table. Each night, as he took in the sight, he resolved that, if he could ever afford another such trip, he would make a point of paying for that luxury. He returned to his cabin saddened. At least, he had the leftovers from his lunch and a few dry biscuits that he had packed in his suitcase for times like these.

The three weeks ended and he was disembarking from the boat when he met the Captain. The Captain was recognisable as he had seen him each night at the head of the banqueting table. "Did you have a good trip with us ?" asked the Captain. "Oh, yes", said the young man, "but I sure would have loved to have been able to afford that delicious looking banquet provided each night." The Captain looked at the young man with raised eyebrows and said "but you had already paid for the banquet when you paid the price for your ticket."

The young man had been so excited and enthusiastic about his trip that he had not even taken the time to read all the small print on the ticket. He did not know all the benefits, conditions, guarantees and promises that were included in the price that he had paid. As it is said 'Had I known is always last.' If you do not take the time to find out what the Word of God says, you will always be short changed. Do not let this happen to you.

Apostle Paul urged the Corinthians to **"regard no-one from a worldly point of view"**. (2 Corinthians 5:16) As Christians, this applies to all of us. It would serve us well to **"regard no-one from a worldly point of view"**. Our God is no respecter of persons and He loves women just as much as He loves men. Men have no copyright on God's love, God's power or His anointing. There is neither male nor female in the Spirit. The scriptures apply to male and female alike.

You need to know this in order to be as effective as God intends you to be in the Body of Christ and in the world. **"For the eyes of the Lord range throughout the earth to strengthen those whose hearts are fully committed to him."** (2 Chronicles 16:9) God is not looking for perfect people, but those who are faithful and devoted to serving Him. God will flow through any available vessel yielded to Him for His service.

In Israel, the ancient manuscripts had no sentence structures like the Bible translations to which we are accustomed in these days. Often we need to go to the literal translation from the original Greek or Hebrew manuscripts rather than rely completely on a more modern version. Going to the original word used will help you to understand what God said about women.

In the sixteenth century, a group of 600 men translated the Bible into the King James Version. There is nothing wrong with 600 men translating scripture in the sixteenth century until you realise that women in Europe were not recognised as part of the electorate. They were treated as items of property until the early twentieth century. It was then that the fight for liberation and equality for women began in Europe.

In the original Greek and Hebrew writings, what has now been translated as the word 'man' had various literal translations. Among these were : mankind, human being, anyone, male and female, person and whosoever. 'Whosoever', the Greek word 'tis', is the one most generally used in the original scripture writings, especially in the New Testament.

'Whosoever'. God does not leave anyone out of the ministry. **"All this is from God, who reconciled us to Himself through Christ and gave us the ministry of reconciliation: that God was reconciling the world to himself in Christ, not counting men's sin against them. And he has committed to us the message of reconciliation."** (2 Corinthians 5:18-19)

To all, who are reconciled to God by Christ Jesus, are given the ministry of reconciliation. All who believe will lay hands on the sick and the sick will recover. (Mark 16:18) We all have the ministry of healing. We are all to have a prayer and intercession ministry. **"And pray in the Spirit on all occasions with all kinds of prayers and requests. With this in mind, be alert and always keep on praying for all the saints."** (Ephesians 6:18) We are specifically told to pray for all saints.

What role has God purposed for women within the Body of Christ? The Prophet Joel prophesied that **"And afterwards, I will pour out my Spirit on all people. Your sons and daughters will prophesy, your old men will dream dreams, your young men will see visions."** (Joel 2:28) Many Bible translations say 'your old men' and 'your young men' but the Hebrew word used is 'enowsh', which, translated literally, reads 'mortals'. In this prophesy, women were not excluded from spiritual gifts and powers.

This happened on the day of Pentecost, when men and women were all gathered together. **"Suddenly a sound like the blowing of a violent wind came from heaven and filled the whole house where they were sitting. They saw what seemed to be tongues of fire that separated and came to rest on each of them. All of them were filled with the Holy Spirit and began to speak in other tongues as the Spirit enabled them."** (Acts 2:2-4) God is a good God, isn't He? He poured out His Holy Spirit equally on men and women.

Many have already received the revelation that there is enough space in the Body of Christ and in the Kingdom of God for all of us. We all need to come to that point. There was no distinction made between male and female when it came to spiritual things. Calling and anointing by God are neither male nor female. We are spiritually created equal in the image of God although in the natural or physical realm we are different.

Men and women, all together, become the Body of Christ. Each of us plays a special part within the body. Apostle Paul confirmed that **"The body is a unit, though it is made up of many parts; and though all its parts are many, they form one body. So it is with Christ. For we were all baptised by one Spirit into one body - whether Jews or Greeks, slave or free - and we were all given the one Spirit to drink."** (1 Corinthians 12:12-13)

In verse 18 of the same passage, Apostle Paul says **"But in fact God has arranged the parts in the body, every one of them, just as He wanted them to be."** If we are involved in team work within the body of Christ, we must pray that God will reveal to us His arrangement concerning those around us.

God has always intended to use every one that He has available, to win the world for Jesus. Every man, woman, boy and girl. Paul wrote to the Galatians **"You are all sons of God through faith in Christ Jesus, for all of you who were baptised into Christ have clothed yourselves with Christ. There is neither Jew nor Greek, slave nor free, male nor female, for you are all one in Christ Jesus."** (Galatians 3:26-28)

The same thought and spiritual truth is confirmed in Romans 2:11 where Paul says **"For God does not show favouritism."** As a woman, you need to find out what God thinks about you and what your role is in the body of Christ. Our Lord Jesus said **"The harvest is plentiful but the workers are few. Ask the Lord of the harvest, therefore, to send out workers into his harvest field."** (Matthew 9:37-38)

There is much work to do in the world before Jesus comes. Who are the workers that Jesus was talking about ? Why, they are all the men, women and children who love Him enough to serve Him. He needs workers to do the work and others to teach and train them to do the work. We need to understand this. God is in the equal opportunity business and does not discriminate on the basis of sex. There should be no competition in the body of Christ except **"to spur one another on towards love and good deeds."** (Hebrews 10:24)

In chapter 8 of this book, we will look at the scriptural insight and guidelines that the Bible provides about the roles of both the single and the married woman. God has specific instructions concerning natural things as well. We will look at how you can recognise and fulfil your role in the Body of Christ. We will see how God used women in the Bible.

Some people or schools of thought have taken particular scriptures out of context and applied them generally to women. This has resulted in frustration and suppression for many women. Such adversities, tests and trials are found in every Christian life, but God has declared **"A righteous man may have many troubles, but the Lord delivers him from them all."** (Psalms 34:19). As the saying goes, "Adversity builds character".

Some Christians have defined the role of women in their own way. The definitions vary depending on the light of the revelation that they have received and the roles that tradition has set. Many people define the role of a woman depending on their own perception or experience with the women who have featured prominently in their lives.

If someone had a mother who was a home lover and keeper, then that person would tend to be comfortable with a woman who fulfils that kind of role. People, who have had a career-minded or professional mother, are comfortable with a woman who fulfils that role and are not threatened by their motivation.

In other cases, the custom of the land dictates the role of a woman. Those with mothers within the Arabic and eastern cultures have come to expect a certain role. There is almost a stereotype woman and very few take the time to find out what God says about women.

All over the world, in all the continents, some women have been made to feel out-of-place, inferior, discouraged, hopeless and neglected. They feel intimidated in the kingdom of God and in some local churches by their male counterparts. Those whom God has wanted to use in a 'fivefold ministerial' capacity have sometimes encountered a glass ceiling. They begin to wonder if God had not thought out their purpose and role in His Kingdom.

Have they really received a raw deal from God since their treatment is no different from the sexist treatment found in the secular world ? We know that no woman needs permission of a man to be saved, healed, delivered, to live in victory or to walk in the plans and purpose that God has for her. What a woman needs is the wisdom of God and a strong prayer life.

People may be obstructive or refuse to open doors, but God is the one who places before you **"an open door that no-one can shut."** (Revelation 3:8) He promises that **"A gift opens the way for the giver and ushers him into the presence of the great."** (Proverbs 18:16) Wait on Him alone. He is the answer to all your heart's desires and needs. Hidden inside you is a great woman, who can do great exploits in His name. God wants that woman to be set free.

If you are a wife and mother, God will give you the wisdom that you need to get where He wants you to be. You only need to rely on the word and wisdom of God. He wants to release that potential within you, so that you can become the person that you were created to be. The power to unleash you is in your faith. Faith in His word.

The entrance of God's Word into our hearts brings light. (Psalms 119:130) God's Word will lead you out of the dark and grey areas of unscriptural restrictions and hindrances. His Word will bring you into the Light. **"Your word is a lamp to my feet and a light for my path."** (Psalms 119:105) Dare to believe that He will do what He said He would do. Turn your attention from your own weaknesses to His power. **"Trust in the Lord with all your heart and lean not on your own understanding; in all your ways acknowledge Him, and He will make your paths straight."** (Proverbs 3:5-6). Rest in Him rather than in yourself.

The Apostle Paul wrote **"For everything that was written in the past was written to teach us, so that through endurance and the encouragement of the Scriptures we might have hope."** (Romans 15:4) Jesus came to set the captives free from whatever oppression or bondage they were under. He delivered us from the Lordship of Satan. He redeemed us from the curse and, even though you can still see the curse all around you, you now have the choice of standing against it. You have authority over it in the Name of Jesus. It is for this very reason that you need to know what has been written in the Bible.

As you study the Word of God in this book, find out what is really in the mind of the Creator of this universe about women. Find out your role in His Kingdom. Know the Truth that will set you free from mind sets and thought patterns that limit you, discourage you or put you in a box.

Apostle Paul wrote **"Just as each of us has one body with many members, and these members do not all have the same function,"** (Romans 12:4) Just as there are a variety of men, so did God create a variety of women. We all have different functions within the body of Christ.

We realize that all human beings are given at least one talent by God. Apostle Paul told the Corinthian Church that **"Each man has his own gift from God; one has this gift, another has that."** (1 Corinthians 7:7) Some are given more talents than others. Many talents and gifts are developed, while others lay dormant and untouched.

Apostle Paul encouraged Timothy **"Do not neglect your gift"** (1 Timothy 4:14) and **"For this reason I remind you to fan into flame the gift of God"** (2 Timothy 1:6)

This applies to us all. All people need to be encouraged to develop and use whatever gifts and talents God has given to them.

There are three main chapters relating to gifts in the New Testament. In 1 Corinthians 12:8-12, we find out that there are gifts given by the Holy Spirit himself. The gifts of the Holy Spirit are the word of wisdom, the word of knowledge, faith, the gifts of healing, the working of miracles, prophecy, discerning of spirits, divers kinds of tongues, interpretation of tongues.

"Now to each one the manifestation of the Spirit is given for the common good." (1 Corinthians 12:7) **"All these** (gifts) **are the work of one and the same Spirit, and he gives them to each one, just as he determines."** (1 Corinthians 12:11) Notice that, when the words 'each one' are used here, the original word in the Greek was 'everyone'.

Isn't it exciting to know that the Holy Spirit does not discriminate between men and women ? In verse 28, we read **"And in the church God has appointed first of all apostles, second prophets, third teachers, then workers of miracles, also those having gifts of healing, those able to help others, those with gifts of administration, and those speaking in different kinds of tongues."** (1 Corinthians 12:28)

It is God who has placed these men and women in the church, no one else. God is no respecter of persons and uses women just as much as He uses men. Women are not God's second choice.

"It was he (Jesus) **who gave some to be apostles, some to be prophets, some to be evangelists, and some to be pastors and teachers"** (Ephesians 4:11) Jesus did not discriminate between men and women.

We are told that **"We have different gifts, according to the grace given us"** (Romans 12:6) God's gifts are given to whom He chooses. The gifts mentioned in this portion of scripture are the gifts of prophecy, service, teaching, encouragement, giving, leadership and mercy. God has blessed the Body of Christ with all kinds of spiritual gifts. Apart from these gifts, we all have what we call God-given natural talents.

If God does not discriminate between men and women in His gifts, who has the right to do so ? God's grace is simply amazing. His love and respect for His own creation, male and female, is awesome. We need to recognise the power of God through the Holy Spirit in all Christians. We need to acknowledge the gifts that God has placed within each of his children and to **"regard no-one from a worldly point of view"**. (2 Corinthians 5:16)

Every Christian has a ministry. We do not have to wait to speak to a church congregation to qualify as a minister of the gospel of Christ. We can talk and minister anywhere and anytime in the environment in which we live, work or socialize. Jesus told the disciples in Acts and says to the disciples of today, that we will receive power when the Holy Spirit comes upon us to be His witnesses in your own Jerusalem, Judea and then to the ends of the earth.

We need to know what God says about us to be able to distinguish between the truth of God's Word and the lies that the world and the devil try to make you believe. As Jesus said about the false teachers and prophets, **"By their fruit you will recognise them."** (Matthew 7:16) Find out if what is being preached and taught is what God is actually saying in His Word. It is the truth that you know that will set you free.

3   The so-called scriptural controversy

Did the Apostle Paul hate women ? Was he just another male chauvinist ? Is that why he wrote certain verses in the Bible ? Is my role in the kingdom limited to teaching children ? Can I lead and teach men ? Can I lead a Home Cell Group or a Bible Study Group ? Is it possible to be a mother and an ordained minister of the gospel ? Can I be placed in a position of authority ? Can I baptise a new convert ? Can I serve at the Lord's table ? Could I ever fulfil my call to be an evangelist ?

You need to know exactly what God says about you in His Word. Jesus said **"Then you will know the truth, and the truth will set you free."** (John 8:32) and **"So if the Son sets you free, you will be free indeed."** (John 8:36)

Rev. Jan Owbridge, Administrative Pastor in my previous London Church, said, in one of her interviews, "If the truth only sets men free, it is only half truth. If it only sets women free, then it is only half truth. The truth will set both men and women free." One eventually finds out that Truth is like soap. Even when you know it, it won't do you any good unless it is applied. So find out what the Truth is and apply it to your life.

One biblical principle to remember when studying scripture is that **"Every matter may be established by the testimony of two or three witnesses."** (Matthew 18:16) This principle is stated several times in both the Old and the New Testaments. Jesus Christ reminded the Pharisees who challenged him for being his own witness **"my other witness is the Father, who sent me."** (John 8:18)

The apostle Paul said **"Every matter must be established by the testimony of two or three witnesses."** (2 Corinthians 13:1) We need to be sure that the scripture that we read is confirmed somewhere else in the Word of God before we accept it as a rule or a doctrine.

If a verse of scripture is not confirmed anywhere else in the Bible, we must check what the verse said, to whom it was referring, and why it was said. We must let the Bible interpret and establish itself. One must take an overview of the whole Bible and look at other similar situations in the Bible to find out if the principle can be established.

A scriptural fact, if it is a fact, will always be proved by something else, somewhere else in the Bible. That is one way to test sound doctrine. A classic example of a wrong doctrine is the refusal of blood transfusions for biblical reasons. In this case, human lives are lost because some scripture is taken out of context. The phrase **"For the life of a creature is in the blood"** (Leviticus 17:11) has been taken by some religious groups to mean that the spirit of a man is in the blood and hence a blood transfusion is a transference of the spirit of a being.

It is well established that, when the blood circulation in the body stops, the body dies and the spirit leaves the body. The life of the body or the flesh is in the blood. In a number of verses in the Bible, it is written that the life of the flesh is in the blood. Many take this to mean that the life of the spirit of a man is in his blood. People are not able to differentiate between the soul, body and spirit of man. There is still lack of revelation knowledge on this particular point in many Christians. **<u>The life of the flesh is in the blood but the life of the spirit is through Christ Jesus. (KJV Romans 8:2)</u>** The born-again spirit of man is not in his blood, his spirit is alive in Christ Jesus.

Another thing that we must do when reading scripture is to discard all traditions and let the scriptures interpret themselves. As Jesus said to the scribes and Pharisees, **"Thus you nullify the word of God by your tradition that you have handed down."** (Mark 7:13) When it came to breaking with tradition, Jesus Christ was the 'worst offender'. We will see this in Chapter 5 of this book when we look at how Jesus broke with tradition concerning the traditional roles of women.

Probably, we all have preconceived ideas with which we have to deal. Many people have some preconceived ideas before they read the Word of God for themselves. We must be careful to put these ideas aside when approaching the Word of God. We must ask the Holy Spirit to teach us and reveal to us what the Word actually means.

This is one of the functions of the Holy Spirit. **"But the Counsellor, the Holy Spirit, whom the Father will send in my name, will teach you all things and remind you of everything I have said to you."** (John 14:26) **"But when he, the Spirit of truth, comes, he will guide you into all truth."** (John 16:13)

With the guidance and teaching of the Holy Spirit, the Word of God is not hard to understand or dry to the taste. The Holy Spirit helps us to understand the Word of God in the spirit in which it was written. Jesus told us that **"The thief comes only to steal and kill and destroy. I have come that they may have life, and have it to the full."** (John 10:10)

Jesus came to do exactly what He said: to give you life to the full. Not to steal, to kill or to destroy any of the gifts or talents that God gave you in the first place. Jesus came to set you free to be the special person that He purposed you to be in His Body.

Jesus also said **"I tell you the truth, anyone who has faith in me will do what I have been doing. He will do even greater things than these, because I am going to the Father."** (John 14:12) Do you have faith in Him ? We all need to find out and ask the Holy Spirit to help us understand what the scriptures mean. This is especially important when a particular portion may apply specifically to you.

There are two main texts used to convince people that women cannot minister. Whenever there is confusion, there is a scripture taken out of context without it being understood. These particular verses have caused confusion, intimidation and fear in the minds of many people. They continue to paralyse many women who wish to answer the Great Commission given by Jesus Christ to all believers.

The first of the two controversial texts is 1 Corinthians 14:34-35. This says **"women should remain silent in the churches. They are not allowed to speak, but must be in submission, as the Law says. If they want to enquire about something, they should ask their own husbands at home; for it is disgraceful for a woman to speak in the church."**

This text does not contradict the fact that women were free to pray and prophesy in the church. Verse 35 specifically says **"If they want to enquire about something ...."**. In this context, Apostle Paul was talking to wives, since he continues by saying that **"they should ask their own husbands at home."** It does not mention preaching, praying, testifying or prophesying.

The Greek language uses one word for woman and wife: the word 'gune'. One has to look at the context in which the word was used to find out if Paul was talking about women in general or about wives. In several passages, we see that both men and women were allowed to prophesy. **"Even on my servants, both men and women, I will pour out my Spirit in those days"** (Joel 2:29) <u>**"Even on my servants, both men and women, I will pour out my Spirit in those days, and they will prophesy."**</u> (Acts 2:18) **"And every woman who prays or prophesies with her head uncovered dishonours her head - it is just as though her head was shaved."** (1 Corinthians 11:5)

We must remember that Apostle Paul was writing to the church in response to information that he had received, regarding quarrels between some saints. He wrote to explain to them some rules of order, doctrine and conduct, within their particular church.

It was the tradition in those early churches for men and women to sit in different sections. It might not be obvious to us today that the wives would whisper and shout to their husbands in another section, if there was a point that they did not understand or if there was a comment that a wife wanted to make to her husband. This led to the noise and confusion that Paul addressed in those verses. I am sure that, unless admonished, I might have done the same thing myself in those days.

It was the same Paul who, in the book of Galatians, wrote that " .. in Christ there is neither male nor female.." (Galatians 3:28) Certainly, he would not be contradicting himself in these two letters about the position of women in the local church.

We must look at the customs of the time and the seating arrangements in those churches. Funnily enough, 1 Corinthians 14 is the same chapter used by many to deny that praying in tongues and other things of the spirit are appropriate today.

Some people wonder why there are mighty miracles and signs and wonders in congregations where the gospel of Jesus Christ is not preached in its entirety or where some false doctrines exist. Jesus promised that signs and wonders will follow those that believe. This is why, even in churches that do not allow speaking in tongues or the laying on of hands, some signs and wonders still follow the Word that Is preached.

If salvation is preached, souls will be saved. If healing is preached, people will be healed. If deliverance from spiritual, emotional or mental oppression is preached, deliverance will come. If prosperity is preached, people will be prosperous. The faith level of the saints is built up by hearing the Word of God, because "Faith comes by hearing and hearing by the Word of God."

God is faithful to His Word. The psalmist confirms that God has exalted above all things His name and His word. (Psalms 138:2) God will always keep His Word, not yours or mine. The anointing of God is on His word. We should speak God's Word always and agree with what He says about us and about everything else.

The Prophet Isaiah said **"so is my word that goes out from my mouth: it will not return to me empty, but will accomplish what I desire and achieve the purpose for which I sent it."** (Isaiah 55:11) In churches that do not allow or encourage women to minister from the pulpit, signs and wonders will still follow the Word of God that is preached.

Some argue that, if that is the case, why should women be given the opportunity to minister, teach and preach ? The reason why this particular topic needs to be addressed, discussed and published everywhere is so that women captives will be set free to do and be what Jesus set us free to do and be.

Why limit the body of Christ to fifty per cent of its potential ? With teaching the revelation of God's word and encouragement, we can strive to attain our maximum potential, building each other up in the spirit. Only Jesus Christ was given the Holy Spirit without measure. We are His body and each of us has been given the measure of faith according to Romans 12:1-3.

We need to work together, being part of one body, to achieve our full measure.

No one can do without the other. For this reason, we need to encourage one another to fulfil their special role in the Body of Christ. When we all work together, we will begin to see ministries functioning in the fullness of their callings. We will begin to see manifestations of the Holy Spirit in full measure. Jesus will be seen in His fullness by the world and by believers as we have never seen Him before.

Ephesians 4:13 says that it is when **"we all reach unity in the faith and in the knowledge of the Son of God and become mature,"** that we will attain to the whole measure of the fullness of Christ. Preconceived ideas, the traditions of man and religion, have to be dealt with in the minds of both male and female to enable the Spirit of God to flow freely throughout the earth, in our homes, in our local churches and everywhere.

Leaders ought to check themselves continually to see if the spirit of control or fear is operating in their lives. If this is the case, it will affect those entrusted to them by the Holy Spirit. Leaders are accountable to God for those under them. They are responsible for the spiritual growth and development of all Christians.

Do not get upset because you feel that some Christian brothers and sisters have not received the revelation that you have received, even when they are in positions of authority. Pray for them. **"Love is patient, love is kind."** (1 Corinthians 13:4) Be patient with them. **"But by faith we eagerly await through the Spirit the righteousness for which we hope."** (Galatians 5:5)

So love them, knowing that it is your faith that overcomes anything that is not of God. If God cannot use you in that situation, He will move you to where you can be effective. Until God moves you, encourage, love and serve. It is God who will open the door for you. You can disagree with someone but still stay friends with them. It is **"Not by might nor by power, but by my Spirit, says the Lord Almighty."** (Zechariah 4:6)

28

The second controversial verse that has caused much confusion for many in the Body of Christ, both men and women, is found in 1 Timothy 2 verses 11 and 12. In his letter to Brother Timothy, Apostle Paul wrote **"A woman should learn in quietness and full submission."** Note the verb used in this verse: to learn.

Verse 12 says **"I do not permit a woman to teach or to have authority over a man; she must be silent."** Here, Apostle Paul is saying that women should not dictate to men. Obviously, he had set up his authority in the church that Timothy was in and he wanted to keep it that way.

In Chapter 6 of this book, we will see that women did fulfil their duty to teach, prophesy, or preach, pray and do other things without usurping authority. In the tradition of the Middle East, it was never normal for a woman to teach a man. Custom demanded that Jewish boys be taught theology and girls how to keep house.

In the cultures in which we live, where there are equal educational opportunities for all, we must respect the expertise of another, whether male or female. It would be silly to turn down a brain operation because the surgeon was a woman or on an air flight because the pilot happened to be female. God is the one who gives the gifts and talents. He places us in the Body of Christ where He knows that we can function best.

If you have a problem with a female teacher, preacher, apostle or prophetess, talk to God. After all, it is He who calls. We learn in the Word of God that **"No-one from the east or the west or from the desert can exalt a man. But it is God who judges: He brings one down, he exalts another."** So we all wait on God to promote us in His time. God is the one who opens doors that no man can close.

In 1 Timothy 2:12, women were being advised not to take over authority that had been given rightfully to a man. Obviously, if a woman had been given authority, I assume that the same would have applied equally : that a man should not usurp authority lawfully given to a woman.

Reading from the words of encouragement that the Apostle Paul gave to Brother Timothy, we can draw a number of inferences. Paul advised Timothy **"Don't let anyone look down on you because you are young, but set an example for the believers in speech, in life, in love, in faith and in purity."** (1 Timothy 4:12) He reminded him that **"For God did not give us a spirit of timidity, but a spirit of power, of love and of self-discipline."** (2 Timothy 1:7)

He told him not to neglect his gift but to stir it up. It is quite possible that there were some women trying to usurp Brother Timothy's authority if he was not as dynamic as Apostle Paul was.

God has set up His principles and guidelines of authority, which we will consider in Chapter 9 of this book. Within the body of Christ, we have to recognise the rank and file of God's army. Rightful authority is given either by God or by man. In the world system, unless the authority is given by the people democratically, it is usurped either by the army, a rebellious group or a dictatorship.

We need to recognise the authorities that God places around us and respect them. **"Trust in the Lord with all your heart and lean not on your own understanding; in all your ways acknowledge him, and he will make your paths straight."** (Proverbs 3:5-6) The Bible says that your gift will make way for you, so keep trusting God and keep faithful and close to the Holy Spirit.

What was the custom at the time that Apostle Paul was speaking ? It was customary for the men to speak up in public assemblies to ask questions. They might even interrupt the speaker when they did not understand anything, but this liberty was not granted to women. What Paul was saying here was that the traditions in which they were operating were not to be ended but they were to be maintained for the purpose of order.

Obviously, women could be appointed in positions of authority, as we will see in some of the later chapters. It is very likely that there was a lot that women had to learn in the New Testament churches, whether they were from Jewish or from Gentile backgrounds.

One of the main reasons why it is important for each of us to know what the Bible says is because the devil knows the Word of God very well. He will quote it to you as he did to Jesus. **"If you are the Son of God, he said, throw yourself down. For it is written: He will command his angels concerning you, and they will lift you up in their hands, so that you will not strike your foot against a stone."** (Matthew 4:6) The devil actually quoted scripture.

What did Jesus do ? He just quoted scripture right back at the devil. Jesus said **"It is also written: Do not put the Lord your God to the test."** (Matthew 4:7) If you are ignorant, you will be playing way out of your league. You will not know what to do when someone throws a verse of scripture at you, out of context.

Does God have a plan for you ? What is the plan ? There is only one way to find out. Read His Word. The Bible never contradicts itself. If it does not make sense, just keep reading. It will soon make sense, when the Holy Spirit has revealed the Truth of the Word to you.

You need to know who God is and what His personality is. You need to spend time in His presence and in His Word to get to know Him intimately. Getting to know His voice and His heart. God is a Good God, a Just God, a Loving God, a Faithful God and a Giver of Good things. Jesus said **"But the Counsellor, the Holy Spirit, whom the Father will send in my name, will teach you all things and will remind you of everything I have said to you."** (John 14:26)

You need to make the Holy Spirit your constant spiritual guide. Be filled with the Holy Spirit and not with someone else's opinions, traditions, doctrines or religion. **"For I know the plans I have for you, declares the Lord, plans to prosper you and not to harm you, plans to give you hope and a future."** (Jeremiah 29:11) God has good thoughts about you. He has good plans for you. Stop walking around in the dark ! Find out for yourself what God has planned for you in His Word. Do not accept the Word of God second-hand. It is dangerous. First-hand is always better.

Is it not great to know that we serve a just, faithful, good, loving, caring God ? No one group of people has a copyright on God's grace, love, His anointing, His plan or the Holy Spirit. Isn't God so Good?

Is it not comforting to know that God created man and woman before He gave them both dominion over fish, birds and creatures. (Genesis 1:27-28). Eve, God's first woman, did not come out of man's foot to be trodden on, but out of man's side to be equal. I heard one preacher say "Man was made out of the dust, and woman out of man, so she was twice refined".

God said **"Let us make man in our image, in our likeness"** (Genesis 1:26). In the next verse it reads, **"So God created man in his own image, in the image of God he created him; male and female he created them."** Both male and female are made complete persons by God in His own image. Isn't this exciting to know ? God created both male and female in His own image. God then blessed them and said to them, **"Be fruitful and increase in number; fill the earth and subdue it."** (Genesis 1:28)

God did not tell Adam to subdue Eve, but told both of them to subdue the earth. Then came the offence that opened the door to sin. Eve, followed by Adam, disobeyed God. She listened to the alien voice of God's enemy and obeyed it. When God spoke, He cursed the man and woman and put enmity between Satan and the woman. That is where the degeneration of humanity began.

Thank God for Jesus, the redemption plan, the power of the cross, and His blood that was shed for us all. The regeneration of humankind began at the cross for all those who believe on the name of Jesus Christ. The funny thing is that, much of the time, women are reminded about the curse that God placed upon them as women. God said **"And I will put enmity between you and the woman, and between your offspring and hers."** (Genesis 3:15)

When we allow God to sit on the throne of our lives, we expect to receive His blessings, benefits and promises. We should not expect the curses that He placed in the garden to continue operating as we walk as new creations in Christ Jesus. The Bible tells us that **"Christ redeemed us from the curse of the law by becoming a curse for us"**.

33

(Galatians 3:13).

When we made Jesus Christ the Lord of our lives, He redeemed us from the curse. The curse is still all around us in the world, but Christians have authority over the curse in the Name of Jesus.

Total and instant deliverance and restoration into a perfect man does not come for most at the re-birth. It comes as we are transformed by the continual renewal of our mind to the Word of God. This takes time as we are changed from glory into glory into glory.

Do men look forward to the reaping of the curses that God pronounced on them in Genesis chapter 3:17-19 ? I do not believe that they do. Did Jesus pay the price for the sin of humanity or did He not ? Does the Bible not say that the promises God made to Abraham are also for his seed ? We are the seed of Abraham. Abraham's belief was credited to him as righteousness. (Genesis 15:6)

When we believe in our hearts and confess that Jesus is Lord and Saviour of our lives, we are made righteous. I believe that the price for all sin was paid at the cross of Calvary by the Son of God. That precious blood washed away all sin. Past, present and future sin, if we receive God's forgiveness. God is not holding any more curses over our heads for sin. Women are washed just as clean as men by that precious blood.

Do not let people make you think that you have any curse upon you just for being a woman, when you have been washed and cleansed by the blood of the Lamb of God. You have the authority to stand against it in Jesus' Name. Jesus Christ delivered and still delivers all who are oppressed of the devil, whether it be emotional, mental, spiritual or any other form of oppression.

I was driving home from work, one cool Dutch afternoon, when the spirit of God spoke to my heart: "Just look at God's women in the Old Testament. Just like the men of faith, there were totally different types of women. None of them was obviously perfect, but God was more interested in the attitude of their hearts."

34

I remembered the film that I had watched some years before called "The Stepford Wives" or something like that. In the film, all the women in an American town were re-programmed by a group of men, their husbands, to be like robots. They were given a lobotomy and were programmed in a particular way, to say and do certain things. They were submissive little slaves.

The women who moved into the town met these totally controlled women. They either left the town or ended up becoming like the women of Stepford. I thank God that He is a God of variety. No two things are identical in His creation and that was intentional.

We read in the Bible **"For my thoughts are not your thoughts, neither are your ways my ways, declares the Lord."** (Isaiah 55:8) I am so glad that God is God and that we are not. His ways and His thoughts are definitely higher than ours. You can never get enough of God. He is more than enough. Just look at the different races of men, the different species of plants, fish, animals and birds, the different cultures and the different continents. God is the master genius and creator. He is simply amazing.

A word of encouragement to women. "God created light and said "I can do better", so He made the world. Then He said "I can do better" and made the animals. He saw the animals and said again "I can do better", so He made man. God saw all He had made and He said "I can do better" so He made woman. Then God rested, because He could do no better."

Although under the Law in the Old Testament, no woman had the right to offer sacrifices or to approach God alone, God still used women to teach, rule and minister. The women that God used were not His second choice but His first choice. God could have used a man but, in many cases, He chose to use a woman.

Sarah is spoken about, both in the Old and the New Testaments. Her name means **strong in faith.** She stood beside Abraham, changed her name to Sarah and had 318 servants under her. They were very wealthy in their time. Sarah submitted to her husband. She even went to live with the Pharaoh in Egypt, when her husband told her to do so.

35

When Abraham deceived Abimelech that Sarah was his sister, God intervened on her behalf. **"The king's heart is in the hand of the Lord; he directs it like a watercourse wherever he pleases."** (Proverbs 21:1) God is still in the business of deliverance. He is the same yesterday, today and forever.

Sarah, aged and barren, agreed that Abraham should have a child with Hagar. It was customary for a barren wife to have her handmaid bear children. The children were considered to belong to the wife. We see this tradition repeated with Jacob and his two wives, Leah and Rachel. Abraham and Sarah attempted to accomplish God's purpose this way, by their own power and human effort. Nevertheless, God stepped in and fulfilled his promise to them both.

Sarah is listed in the Hebrews Chapter 11 'Hall of Fame'. She went through the birth process and delivered a child, not because of her circumstances, but because of her faith. She behaved like most of us when we receive a promise from God. First she laughed, then she tried to bring it to pass, by her own power and effort. Eventually, she had to believe that God could work the miracle by faith.(See Genesis)

When Abraham did not agree with Sarah's decision to send Hagar away, God overruled Abraham's authority and told Abraham to listen to Sarah.(Genesis 21:12) What if Sarah had been silent and intimidated by her husband ? We may not have been the seed of Abraham. God supported Sarah and proved that, although a wife is to be in submission to her husband, she is still free to do what God wishes her to do.

Thank the Lord for husbands who are sensitive enough to submit to the voice of God. Some have stopped listening to the voice of God and would not recognise it even if they either heard it loudly and clearly or saw it in black and white.

We see that two contrasting women were mentioned in the 'Hall of Fame', a married woman and a whore : Sarah, Abraham's wife, and Rahab, the Jericho prostitute. Rahab helped to save the spies because she recognised that they were people of God.(Joshua 6:22-25)

Rahab had no husband, she had the whole city. Wasn't that terrible? Yet she decided to take a stand on the side of God's people and hid the spies. She made the decision in accordance with her faith and took action. She believed that God would deliver her when Jericho fell to the Israelites. What did a good clean godly woman and a prostitute have in common? Both women had faith. Rahab was listed because God does not honour morality, He honours faith.

"And without faith it is impossible to please God." (Hebrews 11:6) Rahab is also listed in the genealogy of Jesus in Matthew's gospel. When I discovered that, it really did something for me. Many religious people shudder at the thought of a prostitute in Jesus's family tree. God is the God of second chances. He will give you that chance, even if the world will not. Thank God Almighty for His grace, His Amazing Grace. Our God is an awesome God. Hallelujah!

God will move in your life according to your faith, not according to your experiences. Experiences may leave you sad, disappointed and a bit wiser, but faith in a loving, mighty God will work for you every time.

Miriam is a woman mentioned as a prophetess in the Old Testament. The Prophet Micah said **"I sent Moses to lead you, also Aaron and Miriam."** (Micah 6:4) Miriam was one of the leaders of the children of Israel. She led the praise and worship. **"Then Miriam, the prophetess, Aaron's sister, took a tambourine in her hand, and all the women followed her, with tambourines and dancing."** (Exodus 15:20).

She was a prophetess because she moved in the Spirit of prophecy and spoke a message from God to the people. Some preachers, who want to discredit women, use Miriam as an example. Miriam fell into a trap into which both men and women fall. She could not control her mouth, but neither could Aaron. **"Miriam and Aaron began to talk against Moses because of his Cushite wife."** (Numbers 12:1)

Sadly, it was Miriam that broke out in leprosy and not Aaron. They were both jealous of Moses' authority. It would be interesting to find out why only Miriam suffered from leprosy. Moses, her brother, cared enough to pray for her and she was healed.

A lesson, that we can learn from this story, is that no one should ever speak out against God's anointed people, whether they be men or women.

When Moses spoke to the assembly of Israel, he told the men and women **"Be strong and courageous."** (Deuteronomy 31:6) Jesus says to both men and women **"But take heart! I have overcome the world."** (John 16:33)

The Lord spoke through the Prophet Joel these words **"Your sons and daughters will prophesy, ... Even on my servants, both men and women, I will pour out my Spirit in those days."** (Joel 2:28-29) He speaks to them to edify others, to enrich His kingdom, and to accomplish His purposes through us.

The Prophet Isaiah said **"You women who are so complacent, rise up and listen to me;"** (Isaiah 32:9) He was telling the women to wake up out of their complacency. When you read the rest of the chapter, you will find out exactly what happens when women are complacent. A pretty sorry sight ! We need to wake up out of our complacency and press on and into God.

We read that **"Deborah, a prophetess, the wife of Lappidoth, was leading Israel at that time."** (Judges 4:4) To many, she is a perfect model of a woman. She had a close relationship with God, which gave her great influence among her people. Talk about a career woman, she was one of the judges and was leading Israel. A wife in total harmony with her husband. She ministered as a prophetess.

It is so encouraging to see a woman whose husband was not threatened by the fact that his wife was a judge or prophetess. I am sure that she must have encountered some male chauvinists in her time. As it is said, "many can comment and criticise but few can do better."

Barak, the army commander, would not go to battle unless Deborah went most of the way with him. Deborah walked with Barak to the battle. (Judges 4:8-9) If God could use a woman like that in those days, how much more now when we have a better covenant?

We read about the intelligent and beautiful Abigail and her surly, mean husband, Nabal. (1 Samuel 25:3) Abigail was a woman, not only of great wisdom, courage and discretion, but beautiful as well. God used her to send godly advice to David to prevent him from doing wrong. She seized the opportunity to do something for the Lord. As a result, she was rescued from a terrible marriage and elevated to one of the highest positions that a woman could have in those days. She became the wife of King David.

Queen Esther was a Jewish maiden who protected and delivered the people of Israel from destruction. (Esther 2 to 9) She secured their safety and respect in a foreign land. When the Jews were threatened with destruction, her uncle Mordecai told her **"And who knows but that you have come to royal position for such a time as this ?"** (Esther 4:14)

Esther commanded a fast amongst the Jewish people. She risked her life to save her people. Esther was prepared to do what was right and leave the consequences to God. It is so true that God will not honour those who remain silent to protect their place or position. He will honour those who, for the sake of God and his word, speak the truth, even in the face of great loss.

Mordecai and Esther are examples of loyal obedience to godly convictions. Twice, in the book of Proverbs, it is said that **"humility comes before honour."** (Proverbs 15:33 and 18:12) God honours you when you are humble. Being humble is to submit to God. Many people think that humility is trying to look humble to human beings. That is false humility. True humility is submitting yourself totally to the will of God. Only God can tell real humility because **"The heart is deceitful above all things and beyond cure. Who can understand it ?"** (Jeremiah 17:9)

The Hebrew midwives were the ones responsible for saving Moses from the death sentence imposed by the Pharaoh of Egypt. They feared God and did not do what Pharaoh had told them to do. God blessed the midwives with families of their own. Jochebed, the mother of Moses, made the decision to hide the child in the reeds along the bank of the River Nile.

Thank God for her obedience to God, that delivered God's people. Nothing was mentioned here of Moses' father. Miriam was the sister who watched Moses until he was taken by Pharaoh's daughter. She was the one who made it possible for Moses to be nursed by his own mother.

The story of Ruth tells of the self-giving love of a devout young Moabite woman and how she came to be the great grandmother of Israel's King David. Ruth seized an opportunity and made a mark in history. She made a decision for God. God is no respecter of persons and shows it time and time again.

Another lady referred to as an elder prophetess is Huldah. She lived in the time of Jeremiah and Zephaniah. We read that **"Hilkiah the priest, Ahikam, Acbor, Shaphan and Asaiah went to speak to the prophetess Huldah, who was the wife of Shallum son of Tikvah, the son of Harhas, keeper of the wardrobe. She lived in Jerusalem, in the Second District."** (2 Kings 22:14 also 2 Chronicles 34:22) This is music to the ears. Another woman and wife who was close to the Lord. As Jesus said on numerous occasions **"He who has ears, let him hear."** (Matthew 11:15)

Then there were the group of sisters who proved that God was interested in what happens to women. (Numbers 27:1-7) The father of these five sisters died, leaving no sons. According to Hebrew law at that time, women were not allowed to own property or to have an inheritance except through their husbands. Only men could own property.

The women were to be poor and homeless ; their uncles would have received all their father's wealth. These women were daughters of Abraham. Boldly and courageously, they initiated a meeting to plead their case before Moses. When Moses brought their case before the Lord, the Lord said to Moses **"What Zelophehad's daughters are saying is right. You must certainly give them property as an inheritance among their father's relatives and give their father's inheritance to them."** (Numbers 27:7)

40

God established the law that the father's daughter could inherit the family's share of land. This law also shows the place of dignity and honour that women were given in Israel.

What if the daughters had remained silent ? The sisters took action in faith. Take action in faith. The Word of God says that you do not have because you do not ask, not because you do not deserve. God is no respecter of persons. He has no favourites, although some may want you to think so. We are all special to Him as His children.

Go to God, do not listen to what man says you can or cannot do. Be like Blind Bartimaeus, the beggar at the side of the road. (Mark 10:46) He shouted to Jesus when the religious folk told him to keep quiet. Keep going to God. Talk to God. Let God show you, through His word and by the Holy Spirit, who you are to Him. Do not let anything or anybody come between you and your heavenly Father.

Isaiah's wife was a prophetess, mentioned by Isaiah in chapter 8. She must have ministered to her husband as well as have children. (Isaiah 8:3)

Psalms 68:11 reads **"The Lord announced the word, and great was the company of those who proclaimed it:"** The Hebrew word for 'company' is 'a group of women'. (Please see John Weslers translation and the Amplified version Psalms 68:11-12). God will use women as much as He will use men, sometimes even more. He has nothing against women. No one has a copyright on God's power, love, gifts, anointing or anything that He has to give. God is good. Thank God that He is God.

God does not look at your gender. He looks at your heart. He does not look at morality and good works, He looks at the faith that lives within. We all have choices to make as to whom we serve with our lives. As the Bible says, **"but the people that do know their God be strong, and do exploits"**. (KJV Daniel 11:32)

Let no man place heavy duty requirements on you as a woman. God does not do that. He places the same requirements for ministry on men as He does on women. God is looking into your heart. You are a spirit being and spirits are sexless. The Bible says **"God is spirit, and his worshippers must worship in spirit and in truth."** (John 4:24)

Know no man or woman according to the flesh. Break free from the traditions and limitations of man. Remember that someone else's limitations may become yours, if you let them. See yourself as God sees you. Go into His presence each day and let Him show you who you are to Him and in Him. Let Him fill you with His wisdom so that you can be the overcomer that He intended you to be.

Hannah is another example of how a woman touched the heart of God with her prayers. She was barren but, even in her pain and disappointment, she turned to God. He heard the cries of a hurting woman and delivered her out of her misery. (1 Samuel 1) What if she had given up hope and become bitter ? Faith is what we need to please our God. We need to wait on the Lord and not give up. Wait for God to appear when we cry out to Him in our situations and circumstances.

A popular writing on a woman is found in Proverbs Chapter 31. This woman is normally referred to as the 'Proverbs 31 woman'. As she was a married woman, we will look at her in Chapter 8 of this book.

One thing that we notice about the Old Testament women is that they were unique, special women who exhibited wisdom, common sense, insight, decisiveness and boldness. As we look through the Bible, we see that God never had a problem with women. He simply loved them. Many men do have a problem relating to women spiritually. They do not see them in the same way that God does. They do not understand these counterparts that God has placed here on planet earth.

Some men feel threatened and intimidated by assertive women ; they try to limit, intimidate and control them. Just because problems are not spoken about, it does not mean that they do not exist. We must be aware of things happening around us and not be like the ostrich, sticking our heads in the ground, pretending that they do not exist.

Unfortunately, all over the world, there is still colour prejudice in a lot of Christian churches, not to mention a sexist attitude towards women. We need to handle these problems with prayer and wisdom.

I have heard a lot of people say "I have nothing against woman preachers". But they will only invite prominent big name women preachers because they pull the crowds with their anointing. Other women within their own home ministry are not encouraged within the local church or else they are only permitted to speak to women.

Sure, they can sing, teach Sunday school and serve. They are encouraged to seek preaching and ministry engagements outside the local church. Knowing the truth will free you from the frustration and the confusion around. If God says that He is no respecter of persons, that settles it. No one can change His word. His word is the final authority.

What kinds of traditions do you practise ? What customs and traditions are practised around you or in the local church that you attend ? Is it tradition based on the Word of God or is it just a practice that men have adopted as the right thing to do ? Do you place human tradition above divine revelation ?

"There is a way that seems right to a man, but in the end it leads to death." (Proverbs 14:12) Some of us are under the illusion that 'ways that lead to death' are too far-fetched, but some traditions that we hold dear do not allow God's Will and purposes to be fulfilled. Many gifts and talents are left lying dormant.

Others argue that the ways that they have been doing things so far have been successful. One may be successful, but is it in God's direction, according to His Word ? It is not what seems right to man that matters, but what God requires of us in the fulfilment of His Word. To be able to distinguish between human tradition and the Word of God, you need to study God's Word diligently.

Jesus Christ is going to build His church and the gates of hell will not prevail against it. He will build His church, based on the Word of God alone. Revelation of the Word of God is progressive. The Holy Spirit is constantly leading and guiding us into more and more of the Truth.

Many want to stay in one place and avoid change. Others want to follow the crowd and conform, in order to be accepted by society. Those that do will get no further than the crowd. "It is easier to swim in the main stream than to swim against the current." It takes courage and boldness to stand against tradition that violates the Word of Truth. It takes guts and faith to flow with the Holy Spirit.

On many occasions, our Lord Jesus Christ broke with tradition. His actions enraged and offended many. There were some who were so offended that they plotted to kill him. Some of the traditions that He broke related particularly to women.

Some Pharisees and teachers of the law approached Jesus concerning the fact that his disciples broke one of the traditions of the elders. They did not wash their hands before meals. Jesus called the company of critics "hypocrites", as they nullified the Word of God for the sake of their tradition.

Jesus said that Isaiah was right when he prophesied about them : **"These people honour me with their lips, but their hearts are far from me. They worship me in vain; their teachings are but rules taught by men."** (Matthew 15:8-9). As believers, we must be careful that we do not nullify the Word of God because of tradition, popular ideas or present-day cultural norms.

Luke 13:10-17 relates **"On a Sabbath Jesus was teaching in one of the synagogues, and a woman was there who had been crippled by a spirit for eighteen years. She was bent over and could not straighten up at all. When Jesus saw her, he called her forward and said to her, "Woman, you are set free from your infirmity." Then he put his hands on her, and immediately she straightened up and praised God.**

Indignant because Jesus had healed on the Sabbath, the synagogue ruler said to the people, "There are six days for work. So come and be healed on those days, not on the Sabbath." The Lord answered him, "You hypocrites! Doesn't each of you on the Sabbath untie his ox or donkey from the stall and lead it out to give it water ? Then should not this woman, a daughter of Abraham, whom Satan has kept bound for eighteen long years, be set free on the Sabbath day from what bound her ?" When he said this, all his opponents were humiliated, but the people were delighted with all the wonderful things he was doing."

Jesus called the woman, who had been bound and bent over for years, forward in front of everyone and healed her. She must have had a very low self-image. Can you imagine what must have gone through her mind and heart when Jesus called her ? Her dreams were about to come true. Someone cared enough about her to do something. Jesus dared to set her free.

This was definitely breaking with tradition as there was a latticed screen division in the synagogues, separating the men from the women. This told the women that they were not good enough or acceptable like men. This is the Jesus we serve. Jesus, Our Lord! Ladies - He dares to do what no one else would do.

He breaks with tradition not only to heal on the Sabbath, but to bring a woman to the front of the synagogue in order to heal her. This must have outraged many. Which is the more important ? The traditions of men or the power and movement of God through the Holy Spirit, operating here on earth through believers ?

According to Jewish tradition, the Jews did not have anything to do with the Samaritan people. They were Gentiles, non-Jews. Then what was the Son of God, Our Lord Jesus Christ, a Rabbi, doing, sitting by a well, having a conversation with a Samaritan woman. (John 4:7-29) It might have been more acceptable if it had been a Samaritan man, but a woman !

Jesus was committed to His heavenly Father's purpose and his inner desire to bring this woman to eternal life. Are we as committed as Jesus was, to fulfil the Word and the Will of God, irrespective of the traditions and cultural norms around us ?

Jesus was invited to have dinner with one of the Pharisees. (Luke 7:36-50) As they sat at table, a woman, who had lived a sinful life, heard that Jesus was in the town. She brought an alabaster jar of perfume. As she stood behind Jesus, she began to wet his feet with her tears. This lady then wiped His feet with her hair, kissed them and poured perfume on them.

In one Bible commentary, it is written "By weeping in prayer and faith, believers express to God what is in their hearts ; such tears are valued as an offering and service to him." (Psalms 126:5-6 ; 2 Corinthians 2:4; Acts 20:19 and 20:31)

The Pharisee said to himself, if Jesus really was a prophet, he would know who was touching him and that she was a sinner. How often we find people standing in indignation and criticism, missing the whole point when a woman wishes to express her love and devotion to Jesus.

Luke 7 verse 44 reads **"Then he** (Jesus) **turned towards the woman and said to Simon** (the Pharisee) **"Do you see this woman ? I came into your house. You did not give me any water for my feet, but she wet my feet with her tears and wiped them with her hair. You did not give me a kiss, but this woman, from the time I entered, has not stopped kissing my feet. You did not put oil on my head, but she has poured perfume on my feet. Therefore, I tell you, her many sins have been forgiven - for she loved much. But he who has been forgiven little, loves little."**

A very common comment that you hear in various fellowships is "It is not traditional for a person to express themselves in a certain way and so we do not allow it". "They are being over-emotional" is the normal criticism, when someone is demonstrative of their love for Jesus. Many are more concerned about the 'proper' way of doing things than they are about God's way.

Because of certain traditions and religious customs, some people have become without hope in the church. Women have lost hope in the church of today. They have lost their direction, purpose, vision, dream and ideas. Jesus is our only Hope. We need to establish ourselves in Him. Christ in you, the hope of glory. Jesus spoke words of encouragement and deliverance to that woman. He said, **"your sins are forgiven"** and **"your faith has saved you; go in peace".**
(Luke 7 48-50}

There will be looks of surprise and shock in Heaven, when the rewards are handed out by the King of Kings and the Lord of Lords.

According to Levitical Law, **"If a man commits adultery with another man's wife - with the wife of his neighbour - both the adulterer and the adulteress must be put to death."** (Leviticus 20:10 and Deuteronomy 22:22-24)

In John 8:3 onwards, we read of the scribes and Pharisees dragging to Jesus a woman whom, according to them, was caught in the act of adultery. If the woman had been caught in adultery, where was the man with whom she was caught ? According to the law, he should also be put to death.

Jesus saw through the questions of those who had brought the woman. He did not bother to argue, debate or oppose any of the existing law, traditions and authorities. Jesus appealed to their conscience when he asked whoever was without sin to throw the first stone. Jesus forgave the woman and told her not to sin again. Let us learn from Jesus Christ himself and be led by the Spirit of God.

Romans 8:14 says **"because those who are led by the Spirit of God are sons of God."** When we come into confrontational situations, let us learn to listen to the voice of the Holy Spirit. **"... Christ Jesus, who has become for us wisdom from God"**. (1 Corinthians 1:30)

The woman, with the issue of blood, is the classic example of someone pressing in against all odds to get a touch from Jesus. Jesus told her **"Daughter, your faith has healed you. Go in peace."** (Luke 8:48) Jesus did not embarrass the woman for her determination and courage.

Like that woman, we must all press in and receive whatever it is that we need from Jesus. Do not let anything and anyone stand in your way. Jesus is waiting for you to decide to press in until you get whatever it is that you need from Him. Don't let the crowds put you off, press in and through. His plans and purposes for your life will be established, but you need to press in through the crowds.

Jesus did not rebuke women for wanting all that He had to offer. Instead, He always openly delivered, healed, praised and commended them in front of the men, when the women set the right examples. It may surprise some to find that identifying with Jesus is as much a woman's privilege as it is a man's.

The apostle Paul teaches that **"There is neither Jew nor Greek, slave nor free, male nor female, for you are all one in Christ Jesus."** (Galatians 3:28) Jesus came to earth for both men and women. He came to set us all free. He longs for that deep intimate friendship with both men and women. We are joined together, male and female, by our faith in Jesus, who is our hope of glory.

"I tell you the truth, wherever this gospel is preached throughout the world, what she has done will also be told, in memory of her." (Matthew 26:13 and Mark 14:9) Why did our Lord Jesus Christ ordain this ? What did the woman do ? The woman was Mary of Bethany, Martha's sister. She anointed Jesus's feet with very expensive perfume as an act of great sacrifice and loving devotion.

As one Bible commentary explains, "Her faith in and devotion to the Lord is the highest example of what God desires in believers."(Note 4) The Christian faith is, first of all, a personal ministering to Jesus. That is the reason why Jesus said that her act of love would be told wherever the gospel is preached. This example of love and devotion to our Lord Jesus Christ came from a woman. Sisters, do you need more encouragement than that to be totally committed to Jesus ?

Do you remember the scenario ? Mary was sitting at Jesus's feet, listening to His teaching, while Martha was very occupied and distracted with much serving. Martha came up to Jesus and said **"Don't you care that my sister has left me to do the work by myself? Tell her to help me ! "** (Luke 10:40)

Martha was complaining because she was doing the things that women were expected to do, according to their culture and tradition. She was serving the guests. What did Jesus say ? **"Martha, Martha, you are worried and upset about many things, but only one thing is needed. Mary has chosen what is better, and it will not be taken away from her."** (Luke 10:41-42)

What did Jesus mean ? Have you really thought it through ? Are you one of those who have been taught that the woman's role is to serve and not to seek the deeper things of God ? Or are we so busy doing the work of the Lord, attending church services and performing good deeds, that we forget spiritual communion with our Saviour ?

There are so many Christians engaged in active, practical service to God but, as my pastor Rev. Kofi Banful explained, they are 'successful failures.' They are just like Martha, serving and doing what they find to do, but have not sought the mind of God about the plans and purposes that He has for them. Some of them even have a bad attitude to go with their service.

They have not sought God for the special part in the body of Christ that He has planned for them. Many Christians are full of good ideas but do not have the 'God Idea' for their life. How many of us are like Martha sometimes ? How much easier it is when we have the mind of Christ each minute of each day of each week, as we fellowship with Him daily.

Let us take this one step further. What was the tradition that was being broken here ? Do you think that Jesus was making a point when he said that Mary had "chosen the better part" ? What is the better part ? Spending time in the presence of God. For some, it is traditional for men to devote themselves to seeking the face of God for prayer and direction whilst the women do the serving in the body of Christ.

God has a special part for you to play in His body. Some are called to direct service of the Lord : preachers, evangelists, healing evangelists, pastors, teachers. Others may be writers, musicians, administrators, helpers, group leaders, hospitality providers, whatever. Others may be spouses, parents, schoolteachers, business people, carpenters, labourers and so on.

You need to spend time in His presence to receive the anointing that you require, to be what He wants you to be. There is only one way to spend time with God and that is through prayer. When you seek God, people will see the glory of God in your face, as they did with Moses, when he saw the glory and presence of God at Mount Sinai. Moses had to seek God in order to find Him. **"Then Moses went up unto God..."** (Exodus 19:3)

Before Jesus chose his twelve disciples, **"Jesus went out to a mountainside to pray, and spent the night praying to God."** (Luke 6:12) Jesus went to seek the face of His Father.

In Luke 9:28 onwards, we read about the Transfiguration. This took place when **"he (Jesus) took Peter, John and James with him and went up onto a mountain to pray."** Jesus spoke with Elijah and Moses, Elijah representing the prophets and Moses representing the Law. Verse 35 reads **"A voice came from the cloud, saying, "This is my Son, whom I have chosen; listen to him." "**

The major biblical landmarks or events occurred after someone dared to hear God, when someone took the time to seek His face, to spend time in His presence. Proverbs 19:21 reads **"Many are the plans in a man's heart, but it is the Lord's purpose that prevails."** We need to spend time in God's presence to receive the counsel, power and direction necessary to fit the calling that He has on our lives. There is no other way.

Jesus said **"But the Counsellor, the Holy Spirit, whom the Father will send in my name, will teach you all things and will remind you of everything I have said to you."** (John 14:26) **"But when he, the Spirit of truth, comes, he will guide you into all truth. He will not speak on his own; he will speak only what he hears, and he will tell you what is to come."** (John 16:13)

Do not let anyone take the place of the Holy Spirit in your life. The Holy Spirit will lead you into all truth and teach you all that you need to know about what God has planned for your life.

1 John 2:27 reads **"As for you, the anointing you received from him remains in you, and you do not need anyone to teach you. But as his anointing teaches you about all things and as that anointing is real, not counterfeit - just as it has taught you, remain in him."**

How precious it is to spend time in prayer, commune with the Holy Spirit and enjoy the presence of your Father. It is then that you receive growth, blessing and victory in your ministry. Mary chose the better part. So should we.

The reason that so many women in the Bible followed Jesus, loved Him and ministered to Him, is because He satisfied their need for uniqueness so perfectly. Jesus elevated women to the place God originally created them to be, by treating them as peers and joint-heirs with Him of their heavenly Father. He respected them and liberated them from tradition and the law. Jesus is the deliverer.

The devil destroyed woman's authority in the garden, but Jesus restored woman and chose women to spread the good news about his resurrection. He came to set captives free, to give freedom to those in man-made and other prisons. To give liberty to all the oppressed.

"It is for freedom that Christ has set us free. Stand firm, then, and do not let yourselves be burdened again by a yoke of slavery." (Galatians 5:1) It is up to us to remain in the freedom that Jesus Christ has bought for us with His precious blood. Jesus warned us that **"The thief comes only to steal and kill and destroy; I have come that they may have life, and have it to the full."** (John 10:10)

We start the New Testament women with Anna. **"There was also a prophetess, Anna, the daughter of Phanuel, of the tribe of Asher. She was very old; she had lived with her husband seven years after her marriage, and then was a widow until she was eighty-four. She never left the temple but worshipped night and day, fasting and praying. Coming up to them** (Joseph, Mary & the baby Jesus) **at that very moment, she gave thanks to God and spoke about the child to all who were looking forward to the redemption of Jerusalem."** (Luke 2:36-38)

Anna had been a widow for years and prayed and interceded in the temple for the coming Messiah. After Simeon had prophesied over Jesus, Anna came up to Jesus and his family and gave thanks. What dedication ! She continued steadfastly in her ministry for years. She did not keep quiet at the appointed time. She spoke out.

How did the angel Gabriel address the virgin Mary ? **"Greetings, you who are highly favoured ! The Lord is with you."** (Luke 1:28) **"The Holy Spirit will come upon you ..."** (Luke 1:35)

Mary's cousin, Elizabeth, was married to Zechariah. It is written of her and her husband that **"Both of them were upright in the sight of God, observing all the Lord's commandments and regulations blamelessly."** (Luke 1:6) Verse 41 of the same chapter reads **"When Elizabeth heard Mary's greeting, the baby leaped in her womb, and Elizabeth was filled with the Holy Spirit."** The Holy Spirit coming upon all these women! We see that, even as early as this time, the Holy Spirit empowered both men and women associated with the birth of Christ.

After Christ's ascension, the way was opened for all believers to be filled with the Holy Spirit.

In his letter to the Romans, the Apostle Paul asked the saints to **"Greet Mary, who worked very hard for you."** (Romans 16:6) Verse 12 of the same chapter refers to Tryphena, Tryphosa and Persis **"those women who work hard in the Lord."** and verse 15 to Julia and the unnamed sister of Nereus. All these women were Christian workers, deaconesses and prophetesses, who laboured in the ministry of the Word.

In Acts 16, verses 14 and 40, we find Lydia, a business woman. She was saved and opened her home to the saints. This is a great ministry for women. Not all women are called to teach or to preach. It is easier for women to have coffee mornings or Tupperware parties to reach others with the gospel than it is for men.

According to the literal translation of Romans 16:1, the Apostle Paul calls Phoebe a deaconess of the church in Cenchrea. She had a responsible position in the church but was under Paul's authority. Her duties must have included attending to female converts, helping them to get ready for baptism ; visiting the sick and those in prison ; and to attend to all parts of the church work among women that could not be performed by men.

Phoebe was probably the bearer of the epistle to Rome. Paul commended her to the church at Rome, not only as a servant but also as a preacher. He had delegated to her the authority to preach. To me, that means that she was free to minister.

At the beginning of chapter 16 of his letter to the Romans, Paul mentions Priscilla and Aquila. He writes about **"the church that meets at their house"** (Romans 16:5) These two people are always mentioned together as man and wife.

When Paul writes about this husband and wife team, the order in which the names are given must be judged against the Oriental culture in which he lived. To mention the name of the wife before that of the husband was not normal in those days.

Mentioning the wife's name first meant that Priscilla was the leader in the house church. Priscilla was the 'pastor' and Aquila was the assistant. Priscilla could pastor the home church because Paul had delegated his authority to her, not to Aquila. She was the head of the local church in the area in which she lived. Whenever Paul talked about the couple, he referred to them with Priscilla as leader. Priscilla and Aquila are mentioned six times in the New Testament.

In Acts 18:1-3, we read that the couple had recently returned from Italy and were both tentmakers by trade. Usually women did not have a shared trade with their husbands. For a woman, she was certainly motivated. The couple were from Rome. We would normally call them Italian. This explains a lot about Priscilla's freedom to express her ministry openly.

Unlike the Jewish ladies of the time, a born-again Italian Gentile would have fewer cultural and traditional hangups. This period of the early church was before the growth and power of the Roman Church, before the total decline of the role of women in the Roman Church. Priscilla was in fact a foreigner. It is usually easier for a foreigner to be herself in a strange place than it is for a woman, who has grown up within a traditional setup, to break free from the customs and traditions.

Contrary to the opinion that a woman must not teach, we find that Priscilla and Aquila, her husband, engaged in teaching Apollos. **"Meanwhile a Jew named Apollos, a native of Alexandria, came to Ephesus. He was a learned man, with a thorough knowledge of the Scriptures. He had been instructed in the way of the Lord, and he spoke with great fervour and taught about Jesus accurately, though he knew only the baptism of John. He began to speak boldly in the synagogue. When Priscilla and Aquila heard him, they invited him to their home and explained to him the way of God more adequately."** (Acts 18:24-26)

Apollos was himself a teacher, yet his knowledge of the word of God was lacking. Why would Paul allow Priscilla to teach a man in Ephesus ? Could it be that he just had a teachable spirit ? Could it be that men here accepted the teaching from a woman more readily than, for example, the men in Corinth ?

We find quite a few verses that show that Apostle Paul used women in his ministry and that he associated and laboured with them. He constantly commended them and frequently used women in his ministry, but only if they were under his authority, or, in the case of Priscilla, the husband's authority.

However, we have to understand the customs and disciplines of the areas in which Paul ministered and established churches. Paul always adapted to the customs in the areas in which he ministered, for example, having Timothy circumcised to please the Jews in that area. (Acts 16:3) No one has thought of making that a Christian doctrine.

At the time, the idea of women teachers, in some towns and cities, was a sensitive issue. If men will not accept the ministry of a woman, it is not because women are not allowed by God to minister, but because some men will not accept the ministry of a 'woman of God'.

In Chapter 2, we looked at the prophecy of Joel. **"And afterwards, I will pour out my Spirit on all people. Your sons and daughters will prophesy, your old men will dream dreams, your young men will see visions. Even on my servants, both men and women, I will pour out my Spirit in those days."** (Joel 2:28-29)

This prophecy about baptism by the Holy Spirit concerned both men and women. The first fulfilment of this prophecy occurred in Acts 1:13-14 where it says **"When they arrived, they went upstairs to the room where they were staying. Those present were Peter, John, James and Andrew; Philip and Thomas, Bartholomew and Matthew; James son of Alphaeus and Simon the Zealot, and Judas son of James. They all joined together constantly in prayer, along with the women and Mary the mother of Jesus, and with his brothers."**

It says that the disciples went up into the upper room and continued with one accord with the women. Interesting ! Does not that mean that the women were already in the upper room when the disciples came in ? Here we find real fellowship. Men and women in one accord.

In Acts 2:1, **"they were all together in one place"**. This was the same group of people who were together in the upper room in the previous scripture reference. **"Suddenly a sound like the blowing of a violent wind came from heaven and filled the whole house where they were sitting. They saw what seemed to be tongues of fire that separated and came to rest on each of them. All of them were filled with the Holy Spirit and began to speak in other tongues as the Spirit enabled them."** (Acts 2:2-4)

We see here that women as well as men were given Holy Ghost power from on high. They all spoke in other tongues and were empowered for service. Empowered for His Majesty's Service. How often are Christians now really in one accord ? A lot of the time, there is so much unspoken discord, which results in very little happening in the spirit. Is it not hypocrisy to proclaim freedom for all, if I am sitting on your neck and will not get off ?

In Matthew 28:1-8, we read that Mary Magdalene, Mary, the mother of James and Salome, were the first to tell about the resurrection. Women have been spreading the good news ever since. Jesus Christ appeared first to Mary Magdalene before he appeared to his disciples. What an honour !

We see that women were used mightily and played an equally important role after the resurrection of Jesus Christ. Just as Satan stole woman's authority in the garden, he stole it again when the Roman church was established and has continued to do so in many ways until now.

One question that many people ask is "If Jesus Christ intended women to be in 'full-time' ministry, why did He select twelve male disciples ?" The only answer that I have found is this. Considering the cultural and traditional struggle that He knew He would have to face with the religious people of the time, it would have been difficult to dig up the ground of religion and tradition using women.

In accordance with Jewish tradition at the time, women held a position inferior to men. We see this time and again in the New Testament. Even the disciples, being Jewish, would have had an attitude to women with which Jesus would have had to deal. In Chapter 4 of this book, we saw how the daughters of Zelophehad were given an inheritance by Moses on God's instruction.

It has always been God's intention to give women a portion, but tradition has always had a way of trying and, in many cases, succeeding to exclude women from their rightful inheritance. Jesus had to break this stronghold of tradition, which He did. Tradition, however, never ceases to rear its ugly head and has to be dealt with constantly.

When you repent of all your sins and ask Jesus to come into your heart and life as Lord and Saviour, something happens to you that has never happened before. The spirit part of your being becomes born again. You receive a spiritual birth to God, just as you received a birth in the flesh when you were born to your natural parents.   The old sinner, that you once were, has died. **"But because of his great love for us, God, who is rich in mercy, made us alive with Christ even when we were dead in transgressions - it is by grace you have been saved."** (Ephesians 2:4-5)

The Bible says that you become a new creation on the inside.   This means that you become something that you never were before.   You become a brand new person.   **"the old has gone, the new has come!"** (2 Corinthians 5:17).

1 Peter 2:9 tells us **"But you are a chosen people, a royal priesthood, a holy nation, a people belonging to God, that you may declare the praises of him who called you out of darkness into his wonderful light. Once you were not a people, but now you are the people of God; once you had not received mercy, but now you have received mercy."**

You become a king and a priest.   A chosen generation.   For most of us, it takes a while to really understand what took place when we surrendered our lives to the Lordship of Jesus Christ. It takes a while to understand that, when we were born again, the Holy Spirit took up residence inside us.   The Holy Spirit is the one who will teach you all things, remind us of things, guide us into the truth and show us things to come. (John 14:26 and John 16:13)

When we become a child of God, what next ?   The Bible tells us **"Therefore, I urge you, brothers, in view of God's mercy, to offer your bodies as living sacrifices, holy and pleasing to God - this is your spiritual act of worship.   Do not conform any longer to the pattern of this world, but be transformed by the renewing of your mind. Then you will be able to test and approve what God's will is - his good, pleasing and perfect will."** (Romans 12:1-2)

We begin to walk in the new life that God has put within us and not according to our outward mankind. The sooner that we are obedient to God's Word as being the Will of Our Lord Jesus Christ, the sooner that we begin to understand the things of the Spirit. We learn to walk more after the things of the spirit than after the things of the old sinful nature. We understand more and more of the new creation realities and who we become in Him, with Him and through Him.

When we get a clear revelation of who we are in Christ Jesus, it will revolutionize our lives. We begin to find our identity in Christ. You find it by allowing Him to show you your own heart, then purify your heart so that you become the same, inside and out. As we spend time looking into the mirror of God's Word and in prayer, we begin to see who we are in Christ Jesus.

Imagine that a baby Prince was stolen from his crib, when he was just a few months old. He grew up in the home of a poor couple in another country. He knew no other life than a life of hardship and poverty. No one told him that he was the son of the neighbouring king. He did not know that he really had a rich inheritance.

One day, when he was much older and able to read, he was tidying up the attic when he came across a very old letter. Out of curiosity, he read it. By reading the letter, he found out who his real parents were, the king and queen of the neighbouring country. He took the letter and went back to his own land and to his real parents.

He had to change his way of thinking. Change his poverty mentality. Change his inferiority complex. Change his attitude. He was the son of the king. He had to keep reminding himself who he really was. He had to begin to conduct himself as the son of the King.

We have to do the same when we become Christians. The Word of God and the Holy Spirit living within us will teach us daily and lead us into a closer relationship with the Father, bringing us to our true identities. Jesus can solve every identity crisis. We are changed from the inside out, not from the outside in. We begin to reflect on the outside, who we are on the inside. We walk worthily of our sonship. We are children and sons of the Most High God.

Afterwards, you realize that you are a child of the Most High God and a joint-heir with Jesus Christ. A king and a priest. You need to find out what authority and power you have. You need to find out what is expected of you.

Jesus said **"I have given you authority to trample on snakes and scorpions and to overcome all the power of the enemy; nothing will harm you."** (Luke 10:19) By the authority in the Name of Jesus, all believers can confront all the powers of Satan and his cohorts. We learn to wage intense spiritual warfare through the power of the Holy Spirit and to break the powers of darkness in our lives and in the lives of others. (Ephesians 6:12-18 and 2 Corinthians 10:4-5) We fight the good fight of faith using all the weapons with which God has equipped us.

God says **"For I know the plans I have for you, plans to prosper you and not to harm you, plans to give you hope and a future."** (Jeremiah 29:11) What is the mind of God concerning you ? You will find out, as you study and listen to His Word, that you have a Great Commission.

You are to **"Go into all the world and preach the good news to all creation. Whoever believes and is baptised will be saved, but whoever does not believe will be condemned. And these signs will accompany those who believe: In my name they will drive out demons; they will speak in new tongues; they will pick up snakes with their hands; and when they drink deadly poison, it will not hurt them at all; they will place their hands on sick people, and they will get well."** (Mark 16:15-18)

You have authority to tell the good news of the gospel, baptize, lay hands on the sick and cast out devils. Like the disciples, you need to be clothed with power from on high (Luke 24:49). This happens when we receive the baptism of the Holy Spirit. (Acts 2:4) In Romans 5:17, we discover that we already reign and rule in this life as kings and priests. In the future, we will reign with Jesus for a thousand years (Revelation 20:6)

60

Just as a child walks uninhibited and boldly into his or her father's office, so we also can go boldly into the Presence of Our Heavenly Father (Hebrews 4:16). Hallelujah !

The best advice for every woman that I have heard is this : A woman, who wants to achieve, must put God first, family second and allow God to set the rest of her priorities. Then it does not matter how much she attains, she is still walking with God. The Bible assures us that, if we lack wisdom in any situation, we must ask God, who gives wisdom liberally to all men who ask. (James 1:5) In whatever situation or circumstance you find yourself, God has a Word for you.

In 2 Chronicles 16:9, we read that **"The eyes of the Lord range throughout the earth to strengthen those whose hearts are fully committed to him."** Those, whose hearts are fully committed to Him, are the ones who seek His face and His will, committed and devoted to God.

The Bible promises that, as you draw near to God, He will draw near to you. (James 4:8) In John 14:21, we read **"Whoever has my commands and obeys them, he is the one who loves me. He who loves me will be loved by my Father, and I too will love him and show myself to him."** and in John 14:24 **"He who does not love me will not obey my teaching."**

Walking with God and keeping His commandments is a daily and continual walk. Our obedience to God, though not perfect, must be genuine. It is through this that we will experience the presence and the love of the Father and Jesus. Our fellowship with the Holy Spirit will be continual as He leads and guides us into all Truth.

If we stop to listen, a still small voice will tell us to get up and seize the opportunities in front of us, to look for the hidden or unseen talent and abilities in our lives, that could be used for the Lord. If you obey that still small voice, God says in His Word that His gentleness will make us great. We must commit and submit our talents, dreams and desires to God.

Let Him sanctify you, then seize the opportunities that He makes available to you. You alone are responsible for using the intelligence, talent, abilities and gifts that God has given to you. They just need cultivation.

God has also called some women to be in what is called the 'five-fold ministry'. We will look at this in chapter 9 of this book. Their purpose in the Body of Christ is **"to prepare God's people for works of service, so that the body of Christ may be built up until we all reach unity in the faith and in the knowledge of the Son of God and become mature, attaining to the whole measure of the fullness of Christ."** (Ephesians 4:12-13)

The purposes of God for your life will become clearer as you walk closer to Him and seek His face. **"God's gifts and his call are irrevocable."** (Romans 11:29) This means that God's will and purpose for you will never change. As you stay close to Him, He will accomplish all that He has for you.

Simon Peter wrote that true life and godliness come through a true knowledge of Christ. After becoming a believer, Simon Peter reveals the key to Christian growth. He says that, having begun in faith, you need to pursue goodness, knowledge, self-control, perseverance, godliness, brotherly kindness and love. (2 Peter 1:5-10)

This results in your having a mature faith and true knowledge of the Lord Jesus. Christianity, as a life-style, is a real challenge. No-one ever arrives at perfection but we are being changed into His likeness, as we spend time with His Word and in prayer. **"And we, who with unveiled faces all reflect the Lord's glory, are being transformed into his likeness with ever-increasing glory, which comes from the Lord, who is the Spirit."** (2 Corinthians 3:18)

We say with the Apostle Paul, **"Praise be to the God and Father of Our Lord Jesus Christ, who has blessed us in the heavenly realms with every spiritual blessing in Christ. For He chose us in him before the creation of the world to be holy and blameless in his sight. In love He predestined us to be adopted as his sons through Jesus Christ, in accordance with his pleasure and will - to the praise of His glorious** grace, which He has freely given us in the One he loves. In Him we have redemption through his blood, the forgiveness of sins, in accordance with the riches of God's grace that He lavished on us with all wisdom and understanding.

And he made known to us the mystery of His will according to his good pleasure, which He purposed in Christ, to be put into effect when the times will have reached their fulfilment - to bring all things in heaven and on earth together under one head, even Christ." (Ephesians 1:3-10)

When you become a believer, eternity starts for you here on earth. To find out more about your future, your hope and your inheritance after here, read the Book of Revelation. In chapter 1 verse 3 of that book, it says that you can only be blessed.

8   Single woman, Wife or Mother

In earlier chapters, we have concentrated on the spiritual aspect of our being. However, we are three-part beings. Just as the Trinity or Godhead is three-in-one, Father, Son and Holy Spirit, so, in a sense, we were created as three-part beings.

We are spirit, we have a soul and we live in a body. Apostle Paul wrote **"May God himself, the God of peace, sanctify you through and through. May your whole spirit, soul and body be kept blameless at the coming of our Lord Jesus Christ."** (1 Thessalonians 5:23)

God is good at creating things like that. Like the sun, the rays and the heat that you feel on your skin. Or water, steam and vapour, three different forms, but still one substance. The real you is spirit. The soul, consisting of our will, intellect and emotions, together with our bodies, form the natural aspect of our beings.

The natural man is ruled by his five senses : sight, hearing, taste, scent and touch. **"For the word of God is living and active. Sharper than any double-edged sword, it penetrates even to dividing soul and spirit, joints and marrow; it judges the thoughts and attitudes of the heart."** (Hebrews 4:12) It takes the Word of God to distinguish between the things of the spirit and those of the flesh or the soul.

We all meet Jesus Christ and make Him our Lord and Saviour at different times in our natural lives. Some when they are young, some when old, others when single, married or divorced, others with or without children, some when widowed and elderly.

Whatever the point of your surrender, God has a plan for your life. Whatever state you find yourself in when you accept Jesus Christ as your Lord and Saviour, however you got there, God has a Word concerning you. He tells you the role that He expects you to fulfil where you are.

Although spiritually there is no distinction between male and female, there are differences in the souls and bodies of male and female. Men are generally physically stronger than women, they have different hormones and they do not carry and give birth to children. Both men and women generally make a choice to get married and to have children.

This is one of the most important decisions that a person makes, whether Christian or unbeliever. This decision comes with its responsibilities and consequences.

The Apostle Paul made a distinction between married and unmarried men and women. He wrote **"An unmarried man is concerned about the Lord's affairs - how he can please the Lord. But a married man is concerned about the affairs of this world - how he can please his wife - and his interests are divided. An unmarried woman or virgin is concerned about the Lord's affairs. Her aim is to be devoted to the Lord in both body and spirit. But a married woman is concerned about the affairs of this world - how she can please her husband."**
(1 Corinthians 7:32-34)

Scripture states that the unmarried state is in no way inferior to the married. The single or unmarried woman is in a better position to offer undistracted service to God without being bogged down with family responsibilities, problems and concerns. They can devote their gifts totally to the Lord and His service. Paul tells us to **"offer our bodies as living sacrifices, holy and pleasing to God - this is your spiritual act of worship."** (Romans 12:1)

Often, single Christians face loneliness and long for companionship. This is where service to a local church or ministry can provide support, with prayer and encouragement to help them in their times of weakness. The Word of God is full of assurances that the Lord is always with us and that we should commit all our ways to Him.

Jesus tells us **"And surely I am with you always, to the very end of the age."** (Matthew 28:20) We are to cast all our anxiety upon Him because He cares for us. (1 Peter 5:7) We are not to be anxious about anything, but in everything, by prayer and petition, with thanksgiving, to present our requests to God. (Philippians 4:6)

When we do this, the peace of God, which transcends all understanding, will guard our hearts and minds in Christ Jesus. (Philippians 4:7) Prophet Isaiah wrote **"You will keep in perfect peace him whose mind is steadfast, because he trusts in you."** (Isaiah 26:3)

Jesus told us **"But seek his kingdom, and these things will be given to you as well. "** (Luke 12:31) These "things" include husbands and children. This is where you need to exercise faith in Jesus's Word and the Bible, seeking first His kingdom.

As the Bible says "without faith, it is impossible to please God", and "the just shall live by faith". One preacher said "faith is the breath of a Christian". You need to exercise your faith and believe what God says in His Word.

In Psalms 37:4, there is a wonderful promise : **"Delight yourself in the Lord and he will give you the desires of your heart."** What are the desires of your heart ? If you are expecting something from God and it is not forthcoming, ask God to show you why. Spend time seeking Him. God has made a promise. He is not mere man that He should lie.

To the unmarried people in the Corinthian Church, Apostle Paul said **"I wish that all men were as I am. But each man has his own gift from God; one has this gift, another has that."** (1 Corinthians 7:7) The Apostle Paul was unmarried and he obviously had a gift for sexual abstinence. But to those who cannot accomplish such self-control, he advised that it was best to get married.

He wrote **"Now to the unmarried and the widows I say: It is good for them to stay unmarried as I am. But if they cannot control themselves, they should marry, for it is better to marry than to burn with passion."** (1 Corinthians 7:8-9)

The Bible says **"He who finds a wife finds what is good and receives favour from the Lord."** (Proverbs 18:22) Yes, the men are obviously supposed to be looking around, so the women need to be praying to be found by the right man. They need to take the time to find out about the men who are interested in them. Get to know the brother. My husband says "Nobody should marry someone that they do not know."

For some single Christians, there is the temptation of fornication to be avoided. Paul told Brother Timothy to **"Flee the evil desires of youth"** (2 Timothy 2:22) and told the Romans to **"Hate what is evil"** (Romans 12:9)

The Bible assures us that we need not fall into any temptation that we are not be able to handle. It says **"No temptation has seized you except what is common to man. And God is faithful; he will not let you be tempted beyond what you can bear. But when you are tempted, he will also provide a way out so that you can stand up under it."** (1 Corinthians 10:13)

Apostle Paul writes **"Live by the Spirit, and you will not gratify the desires of the sinful nature."** (Galatians 5:16) Jesus promises to help you when you are facing temptation. He says **"Whatever you bind on earth will be bound in heaven, and whatever you loose on earth will be loosed in heaven."** (Matthew 18:18) Yes, we bind biological urges, sexual desires and indulgence in such, in the Name of Jesus Christ of Nazareth. We loose will power, self discipline, temperance and self-control in His mighty name.

To some, this may sound absurd, but the Bible tells us to resist the devil and he will flee from you. You resist the devil by using the authority which Jesus Christ has given you in His Word.

A few years ago, I received a revelation of why Paul said that it was better not to marry. Before then, I thought that Paul did not really know what he was talking about. It was at a time when I wanted to win the world for Jesus. I had the Great Commission on my heart and mind. I was married with four children and it was then that I really understood why Paul had made that statement.

I had a wonderful husband and had been blessed with four lovely children. Yet, here I was, with the yearning to jump up and go on a mission. Even though, when I was single, I had wanted to be available to serve God, I had made a choice and a decision to get married and to have children.

This was also a blessing from God. As far as God was concerned, I had a responsibility to my husband and children; after all, God gave them to me. God first, my family next and everything else after that. I then realised that, if the Lord wanted me to do anything, He would have to make it a viable project, task or mission, taking my family into account. My marriage and my children were very precious to Him.

Paul exhorts us all **"Whatever you do, work at it with all your heart, as working for the Lord, not for men, since you know that you will receive an inheritance from the Lord as a reward. It is the Lord Christ you are serving."** (Colossians 3:23-4) Whether you are single, a wife or mother or both of these, you must be diligent, doing everything as unto the Lord.

Yes, our God has a reward system. We are told clearly **"And without faith it is impossible to please God, because anyone who comes to him must believe that he exists and that he rewards those who earnestly seek him."** (Hebrews 11:6)

We must believe in God's Word, have faith in it, and expect the rewards that God promises. If you are a wife and mother, you have to be diligent about God's expectations and the responsibilities that come with those positions. A husband and father has to be responsible for his wife and family and place them before his ministry. The requirement is no different for a woman. Ministry, for a husband or wife, begins in your own home.

Paul tells married couples **"The husband should fulfil his marital duty to his wife, and likewise the wife to her husband. The wife's body does not belong to her alone but also to her husband. In the same way, the husband's body does not belong to him alone but also to his wife. Do not deprive each other except by mutual consent and for a time, so that you may devote yourselves to prayer. Then come together again so that Satan will not tempt you because of your lack**

of self-control." (1 Corinthians 7:3-5)

Marriage is a blessing. **"A wife of noble character is her husband's crown, but a disgraceful wife is like decay in his bones."** (Proverbs 12:4) We saw earlier that a man who finds a wife finds a 'good thing' and obtains favour from the Lord. A wife is a 'good thing'.

We are reminded that **"A man's ways are in full view of the Lord"**. (Proverbs 5:21) God keeps his eyes on us to see how we treat the gifts and good things that He gives us. In Ecclesiastes, men are told to **"Enjoy life with your wife, whom you love"**. (Ecclesiastes 9:9)

One writer put it perfectly: "True womanhood can never be measured by a man's affections or society's praises, but by a woman's own character as measured by the Word of God." We need to look at God's Word and see what He expects of wives and mothers.

When the word 'wife' or 'wives' is mentioned in church, the words 'head' and 'submission' start flashing in the minds of women. In the past, the teaching of the headship of the husband and the submission of the wife has usually been very unbalanced. Verses have been taken out of context and other verses ignored. This has led to many wrong attitudes and much misunderstanding.

For some people, the teachings in this area and the examples seen in the churches have been an obstacle to their coming into the House of the Lord. Jesus said **"Every plant that my heavenly Father has not planted will be pulled up by the roots."** (Matthew 15:13) Whatever teaching is not of God will eventually be uprooted and thrown out of his Body. The truth will always come out. As we have seen in the past, it may take time, but light will surely dawn.

When I married, I made a conscious decision to do so. I chose to commit myself to one man and to serve the Lord together. I chose to place myself voluntarily under the headship of this one man alone. The only reason that I married was because I trusted that God could deal with him. I put my trust in God. I chose to submit to my husband and I knew that, as long as he submitted to God, I was all right.

I knew that, occasionally, he would make the wrong decisions, but don't we all ? I found out that God knew exactly how to reach his heart, so I trusted God. God has not failed me yet and He never will. If I had any complaints, I spoke to God and reminded Him that I was trusting Him. God has never let me down. He has always been faithful.

In an earlier chapter of this book, we saw how the Greeks used the same word 'gune' for woman and wife. The same word 'aner' is used for man and husband. One had to look carefully at the context of the scripture to find out whether Paul was speaking about women in general or wives, men in general or husbands.

In both 1 Corinthians 11:3 and Ephesians 5:23-24, Paul was speaking about the husband and wife relationship, not about men and women in general. In 1 Corinthians 11:3, it says **"Now I want you to realise that the head of every man is Christ, and the head of the woman is man, and the head of Christ is God."**

Some people teach that every man is the head of every woman. That is not right. The Bible teaches us **"But he who unites himself with the Lord is one with him in spirit."** (1 Corinthians 6:17) In simple terms, when we are born again, we are joined spiritually with Christ. When we join our bodies with another in marriage, we become one flesh, but remain members of the Body of Christ. Jesus Christ is always the spiritual head of each member of his body.

"For we are members of his body. For this reason a man will leave his father and mother and be united to his wife, and the two will become one flesh." (Ephesians 5:30-31) When we are married, we become one flesh with our partner, not one spirit. The husband is placed in the natural position as the head of his wife. Christ is still the spiritual head of both husband and wife. Together, they are both part of the body of Christ.

In his book "The Woman Question", Kenneth Hagin wrote "If this were not the case, the wife could not be saved without the permission of her husband." We know that many wives are saved despite their unbelieving husbands.

Paul wrote **"For the husband is the head of the wife as Christ is the head of the church, his body, of which he is the Saviour. Now as the church submits to Christ, so also wives should submit to their husbands in everything."** (Ephesians 5:23-24) Before we consider what the Bible expects of wives, we will first look at the biblical expectations of all Christians.

In the latter part of Ephesians Chapter 4 and the whole of Ephesians Chapter 5, Apostle Paul gives a careful explanation of what is expected of a believer. The basic expectations are :

1.   To be imitators of God
2.   To live a life of love, as Christ did
3.   No sexual immorality
4.   No impurity
5.   To be continually filled with the Spirit
6.   To speak to one another with psalms, hymns & spiritual songs
7.   To sing and make music in your heart to the Lord
8.   To always give thanks
9.   To submit to one another out of reverence for Christ
10.   Wives, to submit to your husbands as to the Lord
11.   Husbands, to love your wives as Christ loved the Church
12.   Husbands, to love your wives just as you love your own bodies
13.   Wives, to respect your husbands.

Isn't it interesting when you look at it this way ? When you put the verses in context, you can see the way that God intended them to be read. God's system or authority is never based on force, but on love and submission - all members being in submission to each other. Submitting, put simply, means giving in to one another in a spirit of love and meekness.

All Christians are called to **"submit to one another out of reverence for Christ"** (Ephesians 5:21) before Paul goes into the domestic relationships of believers. Kenneth Hagin wrote "Most Christians believe in submitting one hundred per cent as long as it is others who are doing the submitting to them. Funny, isn't it ? But, when it is time for them to submit to someone else, that's a different story. All of a sudden, they don't believe in submission any more."

If husbands and wives were submitting to one another in love, out of reverence for Christ, I do not think there would be a problem for husbands to love and wives to submit. Husbands want wives to submit first ; wives want husbands to love first. We are all responsible to God to be obedient to His Word to us. Marriage is not a fifty fifty affair. It is a hundred per cent commitment from the husband and a hundred per cent commitment from the wife. Each partner committed to giving it their best.

From Genesis to Revelation, we see that the Holy Spirit is in submission to Jesus, Jesus is in submission to the Father, yet all three of them submit to each other when it is necessary. Out of this love relationship comes power. You never come across a power struggle between the three beings in the Godhead.

Jesus laid aside his heavenly glory, even though He has always been equal with God. He took on a human nature, becoming like a servant. (Philippians 2:5-7) We must all learn how to submit one to another in the fear of the Lord. Submission is an attitude of heart, which should be prevalent in both women and men. It is only then that God can realise His plan and purposes here on earth.

There can be submission and authority at the same time. This only occurs as equality is recognised. Do husbands accept the fact that their wives are equal to them in the sight of God and that they are joint-heirs with Jesus Christ ? Does the husband accept that his wife made a conscious and voluntary decision to marry him and to accept his headship, out of love ?

Most women really get to know the men they have married after the honeymoon. They begin to find out their faults and weaknesses. Similarly, men get to know their wives. When we marry, we begin to understand what true love really means. **"Love is patient, love is kind. It does not envy , it does not boast, it is not proud. It is not rude, it is not self-seeking, it is not easily angered, it keeps no record of wrongs. Love does not delight in evil but rejoices with the truth. It always protects, always trusts, always hopes, always perseveres."** (1 Corinthians 13:4-7) WOW ! YES ! That is what you meant, when you told him that you loved him.

Before Christ, a woman's submission was involuntary as the result of the curse. Now, with Christ, her submission is a voluntary expression of faith. If a woman submits to her husband and he does not treat her as God commands, then he is sinning against God and his prayers will not receive ready answers. Men are warned **"Husbands, in the same way be considerate as you live with your wives, and treat them with respect as the weaker partner and as heirs with you of the gracious gift of life, so that nothing will hinder your prayers."** (1 Peter 3:7)

Praise be to God our Father who loves us so much ! The world thinks that it is a man's world, but we know that, in Christ, we are all winners. Hallelujah ! God's Word really works. That is why we need to walk by faith and **"trust in the Lord with all your heart and lean not on your own understanding."** (Proverbs 3:5)

Wives are called to submit to their husbands (Ephesians 5:22-24), but that is not their greatest calling. As Nancy Cole wrote in her book "The Unique Woman", (co-written with her husband, Edwin Cole) "their greatest calling is to live a Christ-like life". She wrote that submission is not a sign of weakness. It is a sign of strength. A woman with a strong spirit and strong character can submit best, because she does not worry about the outcome.

She does what is right before God and has great faith that He will take care of her, regardless of circumstances or anything else. Her submission reveals her wisdom. Jesus was so certain of His identity, destiny and dignity that He had no problem in stooping to minister to others in a menial way. His was definitely an act of humility.

Consider Jacob and his decision to leave his father in law. He had the common courtesy to consult his two wives, allowing them to come in agreement with him. In Genesis 21:1-16, we see that sometimes submission requires courage and faith, as it did with Sarah. God honoured her and protected her. As we saw earlier, she still said what she believed, when she had to do so.

Christ is our greatest example of submission. You develop trust in God as you submit to others. You do not need a perfect leader, if you have perfect trust in God.

The ideal wife and mother is described in Proverbs 31:10-31. Living in the traditional setting in which King Solomon lived, with all her servants and money, she would have been able to accomplish all that was described in that chapter. She was a God-fearing woman, a wife and mother, a business woman and a provider. Even today, there are women who possess the virtues of the Proverbs 31 woman, without the servants and the money.

This is how her husband responded to her. **"Her husband has full confidence in her and lacks nothing of value. She brings him good, not harm, all the days of her life." "Her husband is respected at the city gate, where he takes his seat among the elders of the land." "Her children arise and call her blessed; her husband also, and he praises her : Many women do noble things, but you surpass them all."** (Proverbs 31:11-12, 23 and 28)

A wife of noble character is definitely a crown to her husband, but a disgraceful wife is like decay in his bones. As a mother, God expects you to commit yourself to the godly training and discipline of your children. Training is a continuous thing. It is not something that you do once and then stop. It is something that you do until the desired end result is achieved.

The evil worldly influences are constantly infiltrating your family ark. You will constantly need to teach the children what is of God and what is not. The Bible tells us that, if we cultivate in our children a taste for the things of God, when they are older, they will be less likely to go astray and follow the world.

The Prophet Isaiah shared a picture of the peace experienced by the children who had been taught the Word of the Lord. (Isaiah 54:13) As mothers, we need to continually teach our children godly principles and cover them with prayers. Psalms 127:3 says that children are a reward from the Lord. They require wise and faithful stewardship. God will hold all parents responsible for how they treated these rewards that He gave them.

Our first priority as women is our relationship with God. Then comes ministering to our families, our partner and children. After this, there comes our public service to God or what others call our public ministry. This spells JOY. **J**esus first, **O**thers second and **Y**ourself last.

What authority can a woman have ? From where does that authority come ? Is leadership male ? Can women be leaders ? Should a woman pastor ? Are elders meant to be only men ? Can a woman baptise a new convert ? What can a married woman do ? Is a local church to be viewed as a local household and therefore only have a male head ?

There has been and still is much controversy about what women can or cannot do within the Body of Christ all over the world. There are so many differing opinions. As we have established already, the opinion that matters most is God's opinion. After all, He is the one who created us and the one that we worship. What does God say in His Word ?

We have already seen, through the Word of God, that **there is neither male or female in the spirit.** Through the Prophet Joel, God said that He would pour out His Spirit on all people. We have looked at who we women become when we accept Jesus Christ as our Lord and Saviour. We have seen what God has said about us spiritually and the authority that we received in and through Christ Jesus.

We have looked at women in both the Old and New Testaments. We have concluded that God wants to use women just as much as He uses men. God wants to use us all, in one way or another, in His body and in this world. I can never fulfil your calling just as you can never fulfil mine. I can never go to some of the places to which you go.

Most probably, I never speak to some of the people to whom you speak. We are all special and we are called to a specific place and purpose. We need to pray and find out what God wants us to do.

We have seen clearly in God's Word that sex discrimination does not come from God. Treating one sex as inferior was not God's idea when He created Adam and Eve ; it is not so now. Those in Christ Jesus are free from the curse of sin and the law. They have to walk in the newness of life in Christ Jesus every day.

From where does sex discrimination in the Body of Christ come ? If something is not of God, there is only one another place from which it can come. The devil. God does have special guidelines regarding the marriage relationship and the domestic situation.

A marriage relationship is supposed to be a blessing and is not designed to place partners in bondage or under a curse. It is a choice that two people make voluntarily or it should be so. As the Apostle Paul told husbands **"Be considerate as you live with your wives, and treat them with respect as the weaker partner and as heirs with you of the gracious gift of life."** (1 Peter 3:7)

"Weaker" does not mean anything other than that women are built more delicately than men. God, through His Word, has made it clear that each one of His children is special to Him. A king and a priest. An heir of God and a joint-heir with Christ. A member of the Body of Christ with Jesus Christ as their spiritual head.

Jesus Christ is the supreme authority. **"And he is the head of the body, the church; he is the beginning and the firstborn from the dead, so that in everything he might have the supremacy."** (Colossians 1:18)
  "And God placed all things under his feet and appointed him to be head over everything for the church, which is his body, the fullness of him who fill everything in every way." (Ephesians 1:22-23)

When we talk about the ministry, we are usually referring to what is called the five-fold ministry gifts and those in church government. The five ministry gifts are chosen by God the Father and the Lord Jesus Christ in combined authority. No human being does this. Only God and our Lord Jesus Christ can choose and create a minister.

The Bible says **"Now you are the body of Christ, and each one of you is a part of it. And in the Church God has appointed first of all apostles, second prophets, third teachers, then workers of miracles, also those having gifts of healing, those able to help others, those with gifts of administration, and those speaking in different kinds of tongues."** (1 Corinthians 12:27-28)

Also "There is one body and one Spirit - just as you were called to one hope when you were called - one Lord, one faith, one baptism; one God and Father of all, who is over all and through all and in all. But to each one of us grace has been given as Christ apportioned it. This is why it says: "When He ascended on high, he led captives in his train and gave gifts to men."

(What does "he ascended" mean except that He also descended to the lower, earthly regions ? He who descended is the very one who ascended higher than all the heavens, in order to fill the whole universe.) It was He who gave some to be apostles, some to be prophets, some to be evangelists, and some to be pastors and teachers, to prepare God's people for works of service, so that the body of Christ may be built up until we all reach unity in the faith and in the knowledge of the Son of God and become mature, attaining to the whole measure of the fullness of Christ." (Ephesians 4:4-13)

Jesus holds all authority. Jesus Christ sets the ministry gifts in the church and their authority is from Him. Most people do not have a problem with a woman evangelist, prophet, apostle or missionary (whatever you want to call them) or teacher. Isn't it interesting that people should tell God that He cannot call a woman to be a pastor ? We will look at some of the arguments that are put forward.

One argument used is that the local church is a household and a man should be the head of the household. If it were, then God would have had to create an office of a pastoress to go alongside the male pastor, because where there is a husband, there is also a wife and the two become one.

Another argument is that man is the spiritual head of the woman so she cannot be spiritually superior or hold an office or exercise authority that is above a man. I have known husbands who do not feel spiritually inferior just because their wives are in the office of a pastor. They are men who have found their special place in the body of Christ and do not feel threatened or insecure about their wives ministry. The office of the pastor is for the local church and not for the domestic situation. When the married woman comes home, she is a wife to her husband, or should be.

What if her husband is part of her local church but is not called to the office of pastor ? Then he is part of the local body. If there is a problem within the ministry, the pastor takes care of it. If it is a problem that is affecting their home and their marriage relationship, then the wife, like any other minister, has to sort it out and submit to her husband where necessary.

For any wife in full time ministry, the role of wife and mother takes priority over the role within the local church. Many do not realize that, before a married woman will be able to function in the office to which the Lord has called her, her house must be in order or it just will not work.

Some people go as far as to tell God that any married woman who thinks that she has been called to the office of pastor must be mistaken as to her calling, because there is no way that God would have set her in the body as a pastor. Interesting ! Only women who dare to believe God and who are courageous and not bound by a spirit of fear can rise up and fulfil the role to which God has called them in His body. God is the judge of everything and Jesus tells us to judge others only by their fruits. You must be a fruit inspector before you can start making assumptions.

One of the main problems that we find in the body of Christ is when Christians regard one ministry as more important than another. Apostle Paul told the church in Corinth that **"The eye cannot say to the hand "I don't need you!" And the head cannot say to the feet "I don't need you !" On the contrary, those parts of the body that seem to be weaker are indispensable, and the parts that we think are less honourable we treat with special honour. And the parts that are unpresentable are treated with special modesty, while our presentable parts need no special treatment. But God has combined the members of the body and has given greater honour to the parts that lacked it, so that there should be no division in the body, but that its parts should have equal concern for each other."** (1 Corinthians 12:21-25) Paul urges all Christians to **"Be devoted to one another in brotherly love. Honour one another above yourselves."** (Romans 12:10)

In chapter 8, we saw that, within the marriage relationship, the husband is the natural head of the wife. We have seen examples of women that God used, even in the Old Testament, to hold positions of authority. Under the new covenant, God has done and is still doing far more than He did under the old covenant.

Another argument that some use against women's ministry gifts is that men have more authority. That may be true in a sense, when you look at the world and even the church. But it is not authority that breaks the yoke. The Bible says that it is the anointing that destroys the yoke and brings deliverance.(Isaiah 10:27) We definitely need levels of authority in church government, but the authority to the five-fold ministry is given by God.

You do not have to be qualified by man to be called by God, because it is God who qualifies the called. Jesus Christ sets the gifts in the church and, if anyone has a problem with someone called by God, then their problem should be addressed to God. People should not attack, speak against, criticise or complain about whom God and Jesus have set in the body as a ministry gift.

If God calls a woman to any of the ministry offices, she is not usurping authority from anyone. It is authority given to her by God. If God has put the gift in you, it will surely make room for you.

If people, who have a problem with women in authority, were to search their hearts, the Holy Spirit would reveal to them from where their prejudice stems. It could be ignorance, tradition, lack of revelation, insecurity, fear, a controlling spirit or some other influence, not of God.

The Bible warns us **"Don't grumble against each other, brothers, or you will be judged. The Judge is standing at the door !"** (James 5:9) Men, who have spoken against women's ministry gifts that God has set in the Body of Christ, need to repent and ask God to forgive them for their wrong attitude and negative speaking. The same goes for women who have done so. Disobedience to the Word of God is sin.

As we have seen earlier, there are many gifts set in the body of Christ besides the five ministry gifts. **"Just as each of us has one body with many members, and these members do not all have the same function, so in Christ we who are many form one body, and each member belongs to all the others. We have different gifts, according to the grace given us. If a man's gift is prophesying, let him use it in proportion to his faith. If it is serving, let him serve; if it is teaching, let him teach; if it is encouraging, let him encourage; if it is contributing to the needs of others, let him give generously; if it is leadership, let him govern diligently; if it is showing mercy, let him do it cheerfully."** (Romans 12:4-8)

Within local church government, the pastor is the person that God places there to shepherd the flock. The pastoral office is only one of the ministry gifts to the body of Christ. He or she holds the same position of shepherd in the local church that Jesus holds in the universal church.

Apostle Paul said **"Not that we lord it over your faith"** (2 Corinthians 1:24) Some people think that the role of the pastor, or any other minister, is to try to control or exercise authority over the faith of others. The five fold ministry is to prepare and deliver God's Word to the Body of Christ.

The responsibility of the five fold ministry is to **"Be shepherds of God's flock that is under your care, serving as overseers - not because you must, but because you are willing, as God wants you to be; not greedy for money, but eager to serve; not lording it over those entrusted to you, but being examples to the flock."** (1 Peter 5:2-3)

We read that other offices, within the local church, are the office of the bishop, the elder and the deacon. These are offices to which people aspire. In the book of Acts, we see that elders were ordained by men. Paul writes that **"The reason I left you in Crete was that you might straighten out what was left unfinished and appoint elders in every town, as I directed you."** (Titus 1:5)

Paul also writes **"You must teach what is in accord with sound doctrine. Teach the older men to be temperate, worthy of respect, self-controlled, and sound in faith, in love and in endurance. Likewise, teach the older women to be reverent in the way they live, not to be slanderers or addicted to much wine, but to teach what is good."** (Titus 2:1-3)

In the Greek, the word for 'older men' is presbuteros or elder. But, surprisingly, in verse 3, 'older women' is the same word except that it is in the feminine gender. So it is apparent that a church is not out of scriptural order to have elderesses who rule and teach in the church.

These elderesses were not only to be teachers of good things, but were also to teach the young women to be sober, to love their husbands, children and various other things. A church would be scriptural with all male elders, but it would be equally scriptural to have both men and women serving as elders.

Do not be surprised if in some churches you are served by a woman. Women serve communion, teach children's classes, woman's classes, and minister from the pulpit. We find women pastors all over the world. People argue that they are not pastors, but one of the other four ministry gifts.

Obviously, when God calls you and anoints you to function as a ministry gift, you know what He expects from you. People may not accept you or recognise you, but you know what God has ordained. When you stand before the King of Kings and the Lord of Lords, only He will say, "Well done."

In Chapter 6 of this book, we saw the example of Phoebe the deaconess. Paul called her a deaconess of the church at Cenchrea. We read in Acts 6:3, that when the twelve were choosing the first deacons, they said "choose seven men from among you who are known to be full of the Spirit and wisdom." The literal translation of the word 'men' from the Greek language was exactly that. Men, in the male sense of the word. How then can a woman be a deaconess?

Obviously God did not see the choosing of seven men to be deacons as establishing a principle or doctrine, otherwise Phoebe would not have been one. It is the same for any other position of authority in the body of Christ.

I have recently heard of a lady Bishop in America. The Bible tells us that **"If anyone sets his heart on being an overseer, he desires a noble task."** (1 Timothy 3:1) The word 'man' here is the Greek word 'tis'. This literally translated means 'any person'. Many people do not have a problem with female elders or deacons within the local church. They believe that either man or woman can fulfil the qualifications of godliness and abilities listed in 1 Timothy 3:1-7 and in Titus 1:7-9. I also believe that.

The Bible tells us to **"Obey your leaders and submit to their authority. They keep watch over you as men who must give an account. Obey them so that their work will be a joy, not a burden, for that would be of no advantage to you."** (Hebrews 13:17)

Verse 7 of the same chapter tells us **"Remember your leaders, who spoke the word of God to you. Consider the outcome of their way of life and imitate their faith."** Although we are told to obey, watch and imitate our leaders, we should realise that the leadership, under which you are, can keep you from walking in the fullness of what God has promised you.

One writer wrote, "A church can only go as far as its leadership." Your leadership can get you to the promised land in a short time or it can lead you in a circle for forty years, as happened to the children of Israel.

God requires us to be diligent and to study to show ourselves approved, so that we can follow what is correct. Paul told the Corinthian Church to follow him only as he followed Christ. 3 John 1:11 says, **"Dear friend, do not imitate what is evil but what is good."**

Jesus said **"If you hold to my teaching, you are really my disciples. Then you will know the truth, and the truth will set you free."** (John 8:31) When there is a difference between what the Word says and what someone else says, we are to continue in God's word and no one else's.

This is what the three men did in the book of Daniel. God delivered them from the fiery furnace. Whatever the gift, anointing or ministry that you may have, such gifts are no substitute for obedience to the Word of God, whoever you may be.

Promotion comes from God and not from man. If you continue to be faithful in that which you find to do, God will bless you. Jesus said that if you are faithful over a little, He will make you Lord over much. Psalms 37:4 promises **"Delight yourself in the Lord and he will give you the desires of your heart."**

God alone knows the deep secrets of your heart. No one else does. He will give you the desires of your heart as you delight in Him. God is the one who opens doors that no man can shut and who closes doors that no man can open. Whatever doors need to be opened for you, God is **"able to do immeasurably more than all we ask or imagine, according to his power that is at work within us"**. (Ephesians 3:20)

10   Tension in the Body of Christ

In previous chapters, we have examined God's Word relating to women. We have seen, in both the Old and the New Testaments, how God used women. The outpouring of the Holy Spirit was upon all flesh, both male and female, as are the gifts and callings of God. (Note 5) Sex discrimination, as we see it in the body of Christ today, does not originate from God. God says what He means and means what He says. He does not contradict His Word. His Word is His will and His will is His Word. His Word echoes repeatedly that He is no respecter of persons.

Some Christians do not believe that one has to born-again in order to be saved, even though Jesus spelled it out clearly to Nicodemus. (See John 3:3) Others do not believe that Jesus Christ bore our sicknesses on the cross or that healing is God's will for us. (See Isaiah 53:5 and 1 Peter 2:24) Yet others do not believe in the baptism of the Holy Spirit, although they read about the Pentecost experience and the incidents of speaking in tongues recorded in the book of Acts. (Note 6)

A percentage continue to argue that men have more authority in the spirit than women and oppress women in various ways. Whether or not people believe and act on God's Word does not prevent the truth from being truth. Revelation and insight into the Word of God for each Christian and for the body of Christ is progressive.

Are we ready to change our attitudes and move with the flow of the Holy Spirit ? After all, **"those who are led by the Spirit of God are sons of God."** (Romans 8:14) We still have many children in the Body of Christ and very few sons. Many have already received the revelation of the position of women in the body of Christ and are walking in the light of that revelation.

Others merely listen to the word without doing what it says. They deceive themselves. (James 1:22) They know what the Word of God says, agree with it, but do nothing about it. This is what is called 'mental assent'. Faith is more than just knowing what the Word of God says. It is believing the Word of God and acting upon it.

Many still need revelation about the position and function of women in the body of Christ. It is their responsibility to seek revelation from the Holy Spirit to enable growth in this area. Just because you become a father, mother, husband or wife does not mean that you automatically know everything about the role that you have assumed. You need to be taught and learn how to fulfil that particular role effectively. No one should remain ignorant by choice. As the Prophet Hosea said **"my people are destroyed from lack of knowledge"**. (Hosea 4:6)

Having been exposed to men and women of God who encouraged both sexes to reach out and attain the mark of their highest calling in Christ, my spirit was disturbed while on the mission field in the Netherlands. Until then, I had never really appreciated ministries geared to ministering to women only.

Based on my upbringing and experiences, I believed that women's needs, desires and ideas, were dealt with as part of the mainstream ministry of the local church. Where I came from, I had never felt a restriction in the spirit realm. The women were free to express the gifts in them, whether it was in preaching, teaching or any other area of ministry. Men and women respected each other as heirs of God and joint-heirs with Christ. No man was trying to tell a woman that he was better than she was in the spirit realm. It would have been stupid.

While in the Netherlands, I sensed a tension in the spirit. Some men in the ministry were so rooted in tradition and religion that they could not see what the Holy Spirit was trying to do. Many of them no longer heard the voice of the Spirit of God. They were no longer listening and had become unteachable.

Submitting one to another in love (Ephesians 5:21) was something that men did only to other men. All the women were to submit to the men. Anointings or giftings were a substitute for obedience to the Word of God in their own lives and marriages. Male ministers were very good at telling other people what the Word of God said, but that was it. They did not realise that, according to Ephesians 5:28, **"Husbands ought to love their wives as their own bodies. He who loves his wife loves himself. After all, no-one ever hated his own body, but he feeds and cares for it, just as Christ does the church."**

It was easy to see when this was not happening within a marriage. Many men did not respect their wives, but treated them like an appendage : the caretakers of their homes and their children. If a man could not respect his own wife, how could he respect any other woman or treat them in the way that God expected women to be treated ?

I was so glad that the only man, to whom I had to submit, was my husband. These men were so concerned about themselves, promoting their own ministries, building their own little empires, that they did not care one iota about how their wives really felt. They believed in submission, so long as they did not have to submit to their wives in love. (Ephesians 5:21)

Many men were insecure and had such a low self-esteem that any woman, who knew who she was and what she wanted, was not submissive but rebellious. Women, who wanted to minister on the same level as the men, were out of order and a personal threat to the men. Why should a woman want to minister or preach to men and women from the pulpit ? Did they not have enough to do already without trying to be like the men ?

I came across hurting ministers wives, who had not been allowed to express themselves in the special place to which God had called them within the body. Everywhere, I met hurting unfulfilled women. Many felt like prisoners in their own homes. They were held spiritual captives by their own husbands.

In one case, a minister constantly verbally abused his wife. He called her 'fat', never took her seriously and told her constantly that she was 'unworthy' to minister. He continually 'put her down' so that he could feel better and look good. Her spirit was constantly being crushed by her own husband.

As she was a loving wife, she protected her husband's position as minister and did not expose the oppression. She would have been out of order to do so. She knew that, if she did, she alone would still have had to live in the same house with him.

Another wife had been ordered by her husband not to fast, not to prophesy in church and not to lay hands on the sick. Her husband had told her that she had to model herself on another pastor's wife, who was shy and wanted to minister only to children. As long as she stayed married to him and he attended that church, she would have to submit to his authority or be in rebellion.

We read that **"If anyone says "I love God", yet hates his brother, he is a liar. For anyone who does not love his brother, whom he has seen, cannot love God, whom he has not seen."** (1 John 4:20) Jesus Christ left us only two commandments : **"Love the Lord your God with all our heart and with all your soul and with all your mind."** and **"Love your neighbour as yourself."** (Matthew 22:37-39)

This is the one of the struggles that the body of Christ is having in the spirit : many Christian men not respecting and loving women as God requires. They treat women as spiritually inferior to themselves. I came across a young preacher, who had been assigned the youth ministry, when what he wanted to do was to preach. He was frustrated and irritated that he was made to minister to the young ones instead of the adults.

He came to me one day and expressed his frustration about this. My answer to him was "Well, now you know how some women feel when that is all they are allowed to do, even though they are gifted in other areas. God says that he gives grace to the humble and resists the proud, so expect more grace from God." (1 Peter 5:5) There were a few other examples that the Spirit has not released me to share.

I once read a portion of writing by Rev. Buddy Harrison on the 'authority of custom'. It put what was happening in the Netherlands and in many local churches all over the world into perspective. (Note 7) It has a lot to do with tradition. Most of the time when there is custom, it carries authority and it must be observed.

Rev. Harrison wrote "If you go into a church where the congregation does not lift their hands and praise God, you will feel the influence of their authority when you lift your hands. The authority in their custom will affect your behaviour. You may want to praise God, but the custom is ruling. Tradition carries authority."

Obviously, it is acceptable to have custom, as long as people do not make the mistake of trying to put custom or tradition above the Scriptures.

There are various customs that I have come across in various churches that have grieved my spirit. Often, you come across local churches that are no more than 'Boys' Clubs'. The custom was for any serious discussions to be done between the men. There was more agreement between the men and the pastor, than between the husbands and their wives.

There was such a controlling spirit of male domination that it encouraged a spirit of division and disunity between the husbands and the wives. Husbands forgot that such disunity would hinder their own prayers. (1 Peter 3:7) Their prayers would bounce back after hitting heaven's gates. In such places, any woman, who was interested or wanted to be a part of church government, felt that she was out of place.

There were things that you just did not do. Wives were told that they had to have a 'meek and quiet spirit.' What did Peter mean when he wrote that ? In 1 Peter 3:3-4, we read **"Your beauty should not come from outward adornment, such as braided hair and the wearing of gold jewellery and fine clothes. Instead, it should be that of your inner self, the unfading beauty of a gentle and quiet spirit, which is of great worth in God's sight."**

Peter meant that women were not to be more concerned with their outward appearance than they were about their inner selves. They were to be humble towards God and were not to be anxious or worried, but to rest in the knowledge and trust of God's supremacy. Wives were to submit to the Word of God and to their husbands in faith.

Moses is described as being the meekest man there was. **"(Now Moses was a very humble man, more humble than anyone else on the face of the earth.)"** (Numbers 12:3) Being humble did not mean that he allowed himself to be trodden on or that he never stood up for what he believed. Humility, translated from the original Scripture, meant 'gentle in mind'.

Jesus was 'meek and lowly', but that did not mean that He did not do what He had to do. In certain local churches, it was all right for men to openly state that they had a calling as one of the five fold ministers. But that liberty was not there for the women. If a woman did that, she was just promoting herself. She was not 'gentle and quiet'.

How dare you express your desire to preach ? That was something that the men did. You were being rebellious or full of pride to even suggest that you saw yourself behind the pulpit. If you expressed that desire, you were just jealous of the men. In each church that we visited, I could tell which particular customs and traditions were ruling the place.

The behaviour of my husband and myself was affected by these local ruling authorities, sometimes in a very negative way. In one case, we almost became enemies. There was always strife where the ministry was concerned. Thank God that we knew that our marriage was more important than the ministry.

It was all right when the customs did not contradict God's Word. But when they did, I knew that we would have to leave that environment in order to be able to continue to grow in the things that God had for us. If you stayed in such an environment, there was only one thing that you had to do and that was to submit to the ruling customs. In the end, most Christians either lost their spark and fire or they just became complacent.

Many people sit in situations like this and do not realise where they are, because they are ignorant of what the Word of God says. They do not recognise the customs that are not in line with the Word of God. They put their spiritual gears into cruise mode and just sit, without checking God's Word and His Will for their lives.

When a custom or tradition affects the revelation that they have, instead of checking it out and standing up for what the Holy Spirit has already revealed to them, they accept the custom. That tradition is what has authority in their life and not the Word of God.

This is the same problem that Jesus had, when He was walking the earth. Most of the Jews were so deep into religion or tradition that they missed what God was doing, although it was right in front of their noses.

Some think that, given time, they can probably change the custom that is not in line with their revelation of God's Word. Many have tried, some successfully but others have failed. It is said that the spirit that begins a project will continue throughout the life of the project. It is difficult to change something once it has been started and has become part of the 'local culture' of the ministry or the church. It usually takes a miracle.

If you are in that kind of situation, ask the Holy Spirit what you are to do. God knows the beginning and the end of all things and knows what your position is, in that situation. Usually, my husband and I both felt a release to leave that particular place.

Jesus said **"If the Son sets you free, you will be free indeed."** (John 8:36) Once freed from the law of sin and death and the curse and traditions of man, there was no way that I was going to voluntarily submit myself to any form of bondage. When people say that you must do certain things in order to conform, do not believe it, unless you find it in God's Word.

We are to **"Stand firm, then, and do not let yourselves be burdened again by a yoke of slavery."** (Galatians 5:1) Jesus paid a high price for my freedom from oppression and bondage. I would keep it that way. Paul rebuked the Galatians **"Are you so foolish ? After beginning with the Spirit, are you now trying to attain your goal by human effort ?"** (Galatians 3:3)

Both men and women receive salvation in the same way, by faith, but, as they mature and grow, some want to tell women that they can only go so far. Each of us in the Body of Christ, minister or lay member, has to discern between the things of the spirit and the things of the flesh. If you do not, you may find yourself criss-crossing in confusion. Check the Word of God constantly, when you are not sure whether you are doing things after the Spirit or after the flesh.

Submitting to authority in the Body of Christ is voluntary and does not imply a blind response to any order. Submission is a willingness to follow leadership, as long as it does not violate God's Word. Any organisation or local church that treats any woman as being spiritually inferior to men is in error based on God's Word.

As we learn, actions speak louder than words. Do not expect someone to spell it out plainly all the time. If you sit in such an environment, you have only yourself to blame. God gave us all a free will. We all choose which restaurant suits us best. We go to the restaurant where the menu is to our taste. We do not go to the local restaurant, if the menu is no good or poor.

We need to be careful where we eat spiritually. Make sure that you get the best spiritual menu and a balanced diet. God expects you to use whatever talents He gave you. It is your responsibility to make sure that you are serving Him with what He has given to you. Our eyes are always to be on God and His Word, as the supreme authority and power.

When you are led by the Holy Spirit, you will see and sense the devices of the enemy operating, wherever they are. This is why we need to be continually filled with the Spirit. (Ephesians 5:18)

Chapter 11　　　Pressing on towards the goal ....

Jesus Christ told His disciples **"I will build my church, and the gates of Hades will not overcome it."** (Matthew 16:18) Jesus Christ himself, the King of Kings and the Lord of Lords, is building His church, no one else. Solomon reminds us that **"Unless the Lord builds the house, its builders labour in vain."** (Psalms 127:1)

As many labour to build God's house on earth, remember that it must be built according to His pattern and by His Spirit, not according to mere human ideas, plans, traditions, customs and efforts. Anything other than God's Will will not stand. We have taken a deep look into His Word. We see that God intends to use man, woman, boy and girl as part of His victorious army. We have looked at the role of women through God's eyes, as seen in His Word. Where do we go from here?

Knowing that we face strongholds of tradition, prejudice, religion and oppression, how do we women achieve God's plans and purposes for our lives ? How should we react when we come up against opposition? What are we to do about the obstacles and hindrances that we face as we try to reach our dreams and goals ?

What do we do when there seems to be no way forward ? To whom can we turn, when we cannot go on ? What do we do if the road ahead is just too rough and it seems as though you are hitting your head against a brick wall ? Adverse situations have faced each of us at some time or another. Let us look at how some people of God dealt with the difficult events with which they were faced.

The children of Israel were standing before the Red Sea, the Egyptian army behind them and the mighty waters before them. The Israelites **"were terrified and cried out to the Lord"**. (Exodus 14:10) They began to curse Moses for not letting them remain slaves in Egypt. What kind of attitude would you have had in that kind of situation ?

"Moses answered the people. "Do not be afraid. Stand firm and you will see the deliverance the Lord will bring you today. The Egyptians you see today you will never see again. The Lord will fight for you; you need only to be still." " (Exodus 14:13-14)

Moses was fully confident that God had the situation under control. How right he was. He had a relationship with God that, at that time, no one else had. He was the one who dared to seek God's face. Moses knew in whom he had placed his trust. Are you like Moses ? Are you fully persuaded about what God has said to you in His Word and by His Spirit ?

Do you doubt God's Word, when you come up against opposition ? God instructed Moses to tell the children of Israel to move on towards the sea. He told Moses to raise his staff and stretch his hand over the water to divide it. Moses and all the children of Israel had to move forward in faith and obedience.

I am sure that the children of Israel must have looked at each other speechless, as they moved on towards the sea in obedience to Moses. Doesn't this sound very much like our walk with God ? We need to walk on with Him, obeying His Word, fully trusting that God knows exactly what is going on, even if we don't.

King Jehoshaphat was in a terrible predicament. The Moabites, Ammonites and some Meunites were on their way to make war on him. **"Alarmed, Jehoshaphat resolved to inquire of the Lord, and he proclaimed a fast for all Judah. The people of Judah** (men, women and children) **came together to seek help from the Lord."** (2 Chronicles 20:3-4)

After King Jehoshaphat had prayed, the Spirit of the Lord came upon Jahaziel. He said **"This is what the Lord says to you: "Do not be afraid or discouraged because of this vast army. For the battle is not yours, but God's. ... Go out to face them tomorrow, and the Lord will be with you." "** (Chronicles 20:14-17)

On the way to the battle field, Jehoshaphat told his people **"Have faith in the Lord your God and you will be upheld; have faith in his prophets and you will be successful."** (2 Chronicles 20:20)

The praise and worship team went ahead of the army, singing. We read that, as they began to sing and praise, the Lord set ambushes against the men of Ammon, Moab and Mount Seir, who were invading Judah.

King Jehoshaphat's army did not even have to fight. When they arrived on the scene, they saw only dead bodies, lying on the ground. There was so much plunder that it took them three days to collect it all. (2 Chronicles 20:25)

Jehoshaphat waited to hear from God before he moved. He encouraged his people, relying on the prophecy that he received from Jahaziel. We need to wait for a clear word of instruction from the Lord. The Prophet Isaiah put it clearly when he said **"but those who hope in the Lord will renew their strength. They will soar on wings like eagles; they will run and not grow weary, they will walk and not be faint."** (Isaiah 40:31)

How important it is for us to wait on God. This means to trust God and His Word completely. God promises to renew your strength and give you the ability to soar above the difficulties and all the things that seek to keep you down. The eagle inside you will rise up and you will find yourself soaring above the natural circumstances, believing the Word of God and His promises to you. After all, we walk by faith in a mighty God and not what we see happening around us. (2 Corinthians 5:7)

Whatever the situation was, the men of God always sought God's will, His guidance and help. It is the wisest move that anyone can make, since He alone has the solution to every problem under heaven. When you are walking according to His instructions, He will make a way out of no way for you. God says that **"I am making a way in the desert and streams in the wasteland."** (Isaiah 43:19).

Whenever you come up against something that looks bigger than you, find out what God says about it. Approach God. The Bible tells us to enter his gates with thanksgiving and His courts with praise. **"Let us then approach the throne of grace with confidence, so that we may receive mercy and find grace to help us in time of need."** (Hebrews 4:16) Praise God, for who He is and who we are in Him.

Spending time in the presence of God is essential. It is in His presence that we are changed, by the inward working of the Holy Spirit, into His likeness. Looking into the mirror of the Word of God also helps us to be transformed into the image of Christ. You begin to see yourself the way that God sees you. An heir of God and a joint-heir with

Christ.(Romans 8:17) A king and a priest.

The Holy Spirit shows you all the talents and abilities with which God has blessed you. You can identify with others in the Bible. God confirms His love for you constantly in His presence. When you know exactly who you are in Christ Jesus, you will no longer be tossed to and fro. You will no longer be moved by the things around you. Paul writes **"For we are God's fellow-workers"** (1 Corinthians 3:9) Members of the same body. Men and women working together with God for the benefit of His kingdom.

We are to **"pray in the Spirit on all occasions with all kinds of prayers and requests. With this in mind, be alert and always keep on praying for all the saints."** (Ephesians 6:18) We have to spend time in prayer. Jesus made prayer His lifestyle. Some think that Jesus went from one miracle to another, but we see that He went from prayer time to prayer time. The miracles happened in between.

Sometimes prayer is enough. At other times, you need to fast and also pray to find out God's will or direction for a particular situation. When speaking to His disciples, Jesus said **"When you fast"**. (Matthew 6:16) He did not say "if you fast". He knew how important it was, sometimes, to fast. Fasting is not a formula for twisting God's arm, it is setting ourselves aside to receive instruction and wisdom from God. It enables us to be more sensitive to the things of the spirit and to hear what God has probably been trying to tell us for some time.

The Prophet Isaiah described fasting as a means **"to loose the chains of injustice and untie the cords of the yoke, to set the oppressed free and break every yoke."** (Isaiah 58:6)

Seeking God should always be our priority, as He has the plan for your life in His hands. He will set the direction for your life, as you walk with Him.

When you come up against persecution or friendly fire, attack from another Christian, how do you react ? Jesus gave us the solution. He said **"Love your enemies, bless those who curse you, do good to those who hate you and pray for those who persecute you."** (Matthew 5:44)

How difficult it is to do this, sometimes ! Jesus wanted his followers to walk in love always. He wanted us to get to the point of reacting maturely to the attacks that come with being a Christian and ministry. There was a time when I faced what I felt was severe persecution. I wanted to curl up and give it all up. I told God that it was too difficult and that He just did not know what I was going through.

The word of God came to me. Jesus said **"Blessed are you when people insult you, persecute you and falsely say all kinds of evil against you because of me. Rejoice and be glad, because great is your reward in heaven, for in the same way they persecuted the prophets who were before you."** (Matthew 5:11-12)

As one writer explained "Persecution is not the manifestation of hate a person has towards you, but the manifestation of fear that the devil has for you." Heavy duty persecution only means that you have made it to the big league. The devil is trying to take you out of the game. When I realised this, faith rose up in me. The overcomer in me arose.

Greater is He that is in me that he that is in the world. There was no way that I was going to let the devil win this round. I left the pity party and continued my walk in love, focused only on Jesus and His promises to me. I made it through that trial. Again I was more than conqueror through Christ Jesus.

When we face trials, persecution, discrimination, oppression or intimidation, hold on tight to what God has said about you in His Word. That is why you need to study the Word of God diligently. When Jesus told the parable of the sower, he explained that it was the Word in you that the devil wants to steal or to render ineffective. (Matthew 13:18-19)

Every challenge that you face is intended to pressure you into dropping the Word of God. Hold on. Faith is the title deed to that for which you are hoping. Hold on to your faith. God's Word is the final authority on any matter. If God has said it, that settles the matter.

Some people already know what their natural talents and spiritual gifts are and they have been using them effectively. Others are not aware of their gifts and talents. They have not really prayed, asking God to reveal to them what their gifts and talents are. They have not found out what excites them, what they enjoy doing and in what they naturally excel.

God has provided us with a prayer that we can use to receive the wisdom and understanding of His will for our lives and how we are to carry it out. Ask God **"to fill you with the knowledge of his will through all spiritual wisdom and understanding ..... that you may live a life worthy of the Lord and may please him in every way: bearing fruit in every good work, growing in the knowledge of God, being strengthened with all power according to his glorious might so that you may have great endurance and patience, and joyfully giving thanks to the Father, who has qualified you to share in the inheritance of the saints in the kingdom of light."** (Colossians 1:9-12)

Some Christians have never been in an environment where they have been encouraged. Others know what their gifts and talents are, but have not had the confidence or courage to let them out. The best place to develop your gifts and talents is in a small group fellowship, a prayer meeting, home group or cell meeting.

You may never have the courage to prophesy in a large church, but you will be encouraged in a small friendly group. You may never get up and sing in a large church, but you may minister to the Lord in a small fellowship. You may never share a revelation and encourage others in a large church, but you will probably bless those that hear you in a small group. It was in small groups that my husband and I discovered a lot about ourselves and our different gifts and talents.

We all belong to the body of Christ and God places the right people around us to encourage us. He places the five-fold ministry in the body to teach us, train us and prepare us for active Christian service.

Remember that there are five ministry gifts to the body of Christ, not only the pastor. There are the apostle, the prophet, the teacher and the evangelist. Jesus placed them in His body because He knew exactly what we need to train us and equip us to be effective for service.

We need to be obedient to Paul's instruction **"Let us not give up meeting together, as some are in the habit of doing, but let us encourage one another - and all the more as you see the day approaching."** (Hebrews 10:25)

We all need to find a local body of believers with whom we can have fellowship and where we can grow. There are so many areas within a local church into which you may fit. Areas like the music ministry, children's church, the Creche, the teens and youth ministry, greeter or usher, deacon or elder, hospitality team, setting up the hall and tidying up, tape ministry, tape duplicating team, counselling, teaching new converts, cleaning team, cell leader or assistant, administrator, bookstall, looking after the guest list and follow up. The Outreach or evangelism arm of the church, like prison, elderly and hospital visits, ministry to homeless and drug or alcohol victims, or in one of the five fold offices. There is so much work to do in the Body of Christ. There is definitely a place for you, an important part that only you can play.

Whatever your ministry is, you need to ask God to lead you to a Pastor whom you can respect, to whom you can submit and under whose authority you can grow. Do not be a rolling stone, running from church to church, because a rolling stone gathers no moss. You will not be around long enough to get to know the people there and build meaningful relationships with your brothers and sisters in the Lord.

"As iron sharpens iron, so one man sharpens another." (Proverbs 27:17) When you are with honest friends, you become a better person more quickly. Jesus does not endorse lone rangers in His body, since we are all meant to be and to function as a part. If you do not feel comfortable where you are, ask God to show you why. It may be something that could easily be remedied.

You may need courage to approach the pastor or some more mature Christians with whom to discuss things. Pray for courage and boldness to talk about it, if the opportunity arises. Sometimes, an open honest discussion is all that it takes to get you on track, doing what God wants you to do in His body.

"You want something but don't get it ..... You do not have, because you do not ask God." (James 4:2) Do you need a friend ? Ask God for one. Do you need encouragement and support ? Ask God to strengthen you. He will send someone your way. Instead of complaining, grumbling or criticizing, try asking God to make a way for you, if that is what you need.

Ask God to open doors for you to minister in the special place to which He has called you, within the body. God knows exactly where He wants you to be. The Holy Spirit is the counsellor. The Holy Spirit will surely lead you and guide you, if only you ask His opinion and listen to His still small voice. Every one of Jesus's sheep has a sheep pen and a shepherd or pastor appointed over them by the Holy Spirit. (Acts 20:28)

You are not in that church or fellowship by accident. You may be there for a season only, but you need to find out if you are in the right sheep pen. In all things, we are to let the peace of God be our umpire. "Let the peace of Christ rule in your hearts, since as members of one body you were called to peace. And be thankful." (Colossians 3:15)

Once, I was really blessed to hear a teacher of the Word of God share how she had sat in a church for two years, listening to the pastor preach against women's ministry gifts, when she knew that she had been called by God to be a teacher. Like many others and in His own time, God eventually moved her into another fellowship, where she could function in the special place to which God had called her.

Sometimes, wives find themselves in difficult situations when their husbands are not ready to move between fellowships when they are. They feel oppressed, discriminated against, and in prison. I would encourage these women to keep close to God and not despair. Jesus came to release us from any form of oppression and to set every captive free. So keep doing what the Word tells you to do. Love conquers all. Love by faith, if you have to, because it works. Faith without works is dead.

God knows you, knows where you are and knows the plans that He has for you and your family. He says that, if you delight yourselves in Him, He will give you the desires of your heart. Do you believe that God cares enough about you to keep His promise to you ? Do you trust Him ?

As Apostle Paul said in 1 Peter 4:12-13, " ...**do not be surprised at the painful trial you are suffering, as though something strange were happening to you. But rejoice that you participate in the sufferings of Christ, so that you may be overjoyed when his glory is revealed.**"

No situation is permanent. The trials and temptations come with life, but the Bible tells us that God delivers us from them all. (Psalms 34:19) Have faith in God. Faith and patience together inherit the promises of God. Say with King David in Psalms 23:6, **"Surely goodness and love will follow me all the days of my life.."**

God has a special plan for your life and a specific place He wants you to fill within the body of Christ. To help God establish His purpose in our lives, we need to cooperate with God's processes. The Bible does not promise us that the life of a believer is problem-free, a bed of roses.

How many of us have had to go through a distressing situation before, eventually, we cried out to God for salvation or deliverance ? Many have been through traumatic trials, only to get closer to God and onto a higher spiritual level. It is said that the greater the test, the greater the testimony and "adversity builds character". How true.

James told us **"Consider it pure joy, my brothers, whenever you face trials of many kinds, because you know that the testing of your faith develops perseverance. Perseverance must finish its work so that you may be mature and complete, not lacking anything."** (James 1:2-3)

When you come up against a spiritual environment of opposition, strongholds of pride, selfishness, jealousy, intimidation, oppression, controlling spirits, division and disunity, what then ? Jesus gave us the key. He said **"I will give you the keys of the kingdom of heaven; whatever you bind on earth will be bound in heaven, and whatever you loose on earth will be loosed in heaven."** (Matthew 16:19)

Jesus gave us all authority over the power of the enemy. Whatever we allow or tolerate on earth, He would have to allow, since He delegated authority to us. We need to use the authority that we have and bind those spirits that seek to obstruct and hinder the purposes and plans that God has ordained. Bind the spirit of division and the disunity being sown. Bind the controlling spirits.

Paul told Timothy to hold onto the prophecies that had been given to him and, by them, to **"fight the good fight"**. (1 Timothy 1:18) We are not going to cruise into the perfect will and plan of God for our lives.

Jesus faced opposition from the moment that He was born, because the devil also heard the prophecies concerning His life. Moses faced opposition from his birth for the same reason. Do you think that the devil is going to sit back and watch you touch lives for Jesus ? He hates Jesus and so he hates you as well.

The Christian's war is not a physical battle. **"For our struggle is not against flesh and blood, but against the rulers, against the authorities, against the powers of this dark world and against the spiritual forces of evil in the heavenly realms."** (Ephesians 6:12)

We are to put on our full armour of God to withstand the plots and the plans of the devil. (Ephesians 6:13-17) We need to confess the victory, favour, prosperity, health, peace, joy that is ours in Christ Jesus. Jesus said that **"The kingdom of heaven has been forcefully advancing, and forceful men lay hold of it."** (Matthew 11:12) It takes commitment to fight the good fight of faith and to bring to pass God's purposes in your life, around you and affecting your generation.

God has not given us a spirit of fear or timidity. He has given us a spirit of power, a spirit of love and a sound mind. (2 Timothy 1:7) We need to continually bind the spirit of fear that tries to intimidate us and stop us from fulfilling God's purposes in our lives. Use the authority that you have over all the power of the enemy. (Luke 10:19)

The Bible promises us that **"If you are willing and obedient, you will eat the best from the land."** (Isaiah 1:19) Some people are willing, but not obedient. Others are obedient, but not willing. You have to be both willing and obedient.

If, in our lives, we are seeking first God's kingdom and his righteousness, God will make sure that all the godly things that we desire will be given to us. (Matthew 6:33) He will give us the desires of our hearts. As long as we remain faithful to God and to His Word, He can continue the good work that He has begun in us and carry it on to completion. (Philippians 1:6)

We need to constantly check ourselves and our lives. Is there any unnecessary baggage that we are carrying with us ? Any area of sin, compromise, stubbornness ? The lighter the load, the faster that we can run. Paul tells us to **"throw off everything that hinders and the sin that so easily entangles, and let us run with perseverance the race marked out for us."** (Hebrews 12:1)

Do not make excuses for carrying that particular sin. Drop that weight. Sin keeps you from walking in the full blessings of God for your life. Sin does not just hurt God, it hurts us.

No Christian ever arrives completely. We are daily being changed from glory into glory. We will only attain perfection when we see Jesus face to face. Interesting, isn't it ? No one on the face of this earth will ever attain perfection until Jesus comes. This is why we need to be patient with one another, because God has not yet finished with any one of us.

Jesus told us quite clearly that, without Him, we can do nothing. (John 15:5) It is not by our power or by our might, but by the Spirit of God. As you walk in obedience, love and wisdom, God will take you where He needs you to be. We must try as much as possible to move always from a position of peace.

Pastor Michael Bassett always encouraged his sheep to "stay sweet", whatever the situation. You may not agree with someone, but just stay sweet and continue to walk in love. King David said about God **"You stoop down to make me great."** (Psalms 18:35)

God is the one who will take you through fire and water. You will neither burn nor drown. He will walk with you through the valley of the shadow of death. He is able to accomplish all that concerns you, if only you trust Him. The gifts and callings of God are without repentance. God does not change His mind about you or about your ministry. He is the God of your breakthroughs.

God alone can open doors that no man can close. Ask Him to open your doors for you. Do not waste your time complaining or grumbling. Seek His face. Obey His Word. Study to show yourself approved unto Him.

Trust only in Him. He will bring your desires to pass. Yes, God cares more about you than you care about yourself. Remember, He created you. He has your plan in the palm of His hand. **"Commit your way to the Lord; trust in him and he will do this."** (Psalms 37:5)

Afterword

If, on reading this book, you would like to contact the author for more information on any area, including Receiving your healing, the Holy Spirit baptism, meetings, support or sending in your prayer requests, please write or send a fax to :

Suzanne Nti
Love Alight Ministries
10 Talman Grove
STANMORE, Middx HA7 4UQ
England

Fax : 0181 357 4258

Notes

1. Myles Monroe in a video recorded message that he preached in the USA in the early 90's.

2. Edwin Cole in the book "The Unique Woman" which he co-wrote with his wife Nancy.

3. Edwin Cole in "The Unique Woman".

4. "The Full Life Study Bible" by Zondervan Publishing House, Grand Rapids, Michigan 49530 USA. (ISBN 0-310-91693-3)

5. See Galatians 3:28, Joel 2:28-29, 1 Corinthians 12:4-11 and 1 Corinthians 12:27-28

6. See Acts 1:7-8, 2:4 and 10:45-46, 1 Corinthians 12:4-10, 14:5-6 and 14:13-17

7. "Understanding authority for effective leadership" by Dr. Buddy Harrison, Harrison House, Tulsa, Oklahoma, USA (ISBN 0-89274-379-4)

Bibliography

When I felt led to write this book concerning the role of Women in God's eyes, I started on a search for truth. I found some on my own, but I received a great deal more inspiration from a tape message of Patricia Bailey called "Woman, break free".

I received invaluable insight from Ed and Nancy Cole's book, "The Unique Woman" and from a tape message by Judith Rend, ministering to a Women's Conference in the Netherlands.

For a more in-depth study of this topic, Rev. Jan Owbridge's book, "The Word on Women" is a must. (Published by Vision International. ISBN 0-9523408-5-2)

Kenneth E Hagin's book on "The Women's Question" is essential reading for both men and women, but especially for women who feel a strong call of God on their life. (Published by Kenneth Hagin Ministries. ISBN 0-892176-405-8)

I praise God for the ministry of Brother Kenneth and Sister Gloria Copeland who were a daily source of inspiration and learning, through their daily devotional, "Faith to Faith". (Published by Kenneth Copeland Publications. ISBN 0-88114-829-6)

I give credit to Donald C. Stamps, the General Editor of "The Full Life Study Bible", and to Finis Jennings Dake, author of "Dake's Annotated Reference Bible", for their study notes that were a constant aid to my writing.

I give credit to books on Ministry and Church Government by Bob Yandian and Buddy Harrison. "Understanding authority for effective leadership" Published by Harrison House. (ISBN 0-89274-379-4)

Acknowledgment of sincere gratitude

To the Holy Spirit for His continual presence, teaching and guidance, every day of my life, and for constantly bringing the right people around me. To my Lord and Saviour Jesus for paying my debt. May God's Name be Glorified both now and forever.

To my parents, Charles and Betty Quartey, who showed me that all things are possible if you are determined.

To my husband, Danni, for his patience. He brought balance, love and companionship to my life.

To my pastors, Bishop Nicholas Duncan-Williams, Rev. Dr. Michael Bassett and Pastor Kofi Banful, for their example, training, teaching and godly counsel that helped shape and re-shape my life.

To Rev. Ford Pickering, with whom I served on the mission field in the Netherlands. It was there that the rubber hit the road and my writing and other gifts were stimulated.

To Rev. Marcia Da Costa for her sisterly love, listening ears, patience and godly counsel.

To Liz, for her timely dedication and assistance.

To all my sisters in the Lord, especially Febe, Mimi, KK and Ursula, for their encouragement and support, and on whose behalf I write.

To Alick Hartley, my publisher, without whom this manuscript would still be gathering dust on the shelf. He truly was 'heaven-sent'.

To all my family and friends, and Christians everywhere.

To Kenton Photographic Services, Harrow for the superb photographs.

To Impressive Images, London for the excellent design of the cover.

To BPC Wheatons Ltd, Exeter EX2 8RP for their help and assistance in the printing of the book.

"The Tale of Three Dogs"

"The Tale of Three Dogs" is the true story of how the Lord used three young dogs to overcome Leukaemia and Angina and give a new life to one old man. Beautifully illustrated. 88 pages. ISBN 1 874155 13 5

Other books published by IMPART BOOKS

"Basic Accounts for the Church Treasurer"
by
Alick Hartley, B.Sc.

This book is intended to be a guide to the honorary treasurers of Churches and similar organisations in the maintenance of essential accounts. It outlines the **principles** of accounting : details of the accounts will vary from Church to Church.

As an illustration of the principles of book-keeping, the book follows through all the financial transactions occurring in one calendar month in the life of ANYTOWN ANYDENOM CHURCH.

It is not expected that this small book will answer all the book-keeping problems which may face a Church Treasurer, but it is hoped that it will point the Treasurer in the right direction.

The book includes guidance to Church Auditors in the audit of the Church accounts.

The book was first published in August 1988, it was revised and reprinted in July 1990, and reprinted in October 1996.

ISBN 0 9513233 3 4

"Step-by-step Guide for the Honorary Treasurer"
by
Alick Hartley, B.Sc.

This parallel book is suitable for the treasurers of organisations within the Church, such as youth groups etc.

ISBN 0 9513233 1 8

Bible-based Puzzle Books

These Bible-based puzzle books are not only entertaining but also educational. Solving the puzzles requires the study and knowledge of the bible.

"Quotation Quiz"

This book contains 358 incomplete quotations which have to be completed. It provides ideal material for a short quiz in a youth group. The number of words required to complete the quotation is given. To enable the answers to be checked, the references are given at the back of the book.   ISBN 1 874155 11 9

"Search the Word"

This book contains 57 word searches, each word search is on a topic based on the Bible, such as 'Things to get rid of', 'Things of which there is only one', 'Items of clothing', 'Names given to the Word of God'. The number of words to be found is given for each puzzle. ISBN 0 9513233 9 3

"Crossed Keys"

This book contains 20 Bible-based crossword puzzles. Each clue is a reference in the Bible. The word required is the key word of the verse. For example, 2 Corinthians 4:16 'renewed'.   ISBN 1 874155 40 2

"Links within the Word" and "More Links within the Word"

Each of these two books contains 20 'Links', each link is on a topic based on the Bible, such as 'Things to pursue', 'Gifts of the Spirit', 'Things to which heaven is likened', 'Foods'. As a help, scripture references are given below each puzzle.

"Links within the Word" ISBN 1 874155 99 2

"More Links within the Word" ISBN 1 874155 02 X

"Buried Treasure"

This book contains 38 of the most challenging puzzles in this series, each puzzle having the name of a gem, such as Amethyst. You are given a word search, which contains all the words in a verse of scripture. You are also told how many words there are in each of the eight directions. When you have found all the required words, the words are to be fitted into a series of 'boxes' indicating the length of each word. You will then find part of the "Buried Treasure", a verse of scripture. So that you can check on your success, a list of the scripture verses - in Bible order - is given at the back of the book. ISBN 1 874155 00 3

From the Office of the Presiding Bishop of C A F M International
Bishop Nicholas Duncan-Williams

"God's Call to Women"

The Book

Are you a woman desiring to be chosen and used of God ? Or a man wishing to understand God's true role of women in His kingdom ? Then this is the book which I recommend would lift you out of the age-old traditions and long time misinterpretations of who the woman of God truly is.

This book could serve as a handbook, a study material or a motivational emancipator for numerous women in need of practical and scripturally based solutions to serving in the Ministry.

"God's Call to Women" is long awaited and a certain must-read which will encourage women to fulfil their true position in Christ. It successfully follows a rhythmic pattern of information, revelation, argumentation and ideas designed to bring insight, healing and deliverance to all who are in search of true service, but who have not been permitted to fulfil the call and purpose of God on their life. It carries the woman from the beginning of the problem by asking those impossible and difficult questions, and also offers her the answers which few have ventured to address like scriptural controversies, breaking of tradition and defining of the various roles of women in relation to their men, themselves and God.

'A true eye-opener and an inspiration to all who are willing to yield with their hearts and minds.'

The Author

I have known Mrs Suzanne Nti for over ten years, during which time I have related to her in the capacity of older brother, father and boss. She was the first and is the present Administrator of the London Headquarters of CAFM. A qualified lawyer with a strong business background.

I have seen Suzanne pass through times of sorrow and hardship for the Kingdom. Paralysed by Gianne Barre Syndrome, I have witnessed God's hand in her total healing. Her sheer determination to return to the cutting edge of service in God's Ministry is highly commendable. I have every confidence that all the experiences shared in this book are well founded and clearly understood by her, therefore making her a voice and a mouth-piece for the women in her time and generation.

Together with her husband, Daniel, they have four beautiful and prophetic children, Rhema (Revelation), Aman (Believe), Rock (Jesus our Rock) and Judah (Praise).

Bishop Nicholas Duncan-Williams
Founder & President of CAFM International.
11 September 1996

CAFM is the abbreviation for **Christian Action Faith Ministry.**